BE SOMEONE

BE SOMEONE

OPERATIONALIZE VISION TO MAKE AN IMPACT IN LIFE, BUSINESS AND THE WORLD.

ADAM JORDAN ARAFAT

NEW DEGREE PRESS

BE SOMEONE

Operationalize Vision to Make an Impact in Life, Business and the World.

ISBN   978-1-63676-500-6 *Paperback*

           978-1-63676-014-8 *Kindle Ebook*

           978-1-63676-015-5 *Ebook*

To everyone who mentored, listened, contributed,
shared my message, and believed in me, thank you
so much for joining me on this book-writing journey;
without you this book would not exist today.

CONTENTS

AUTHOR'S NOTE

———

The writing of this book started out of a need. In university we were prepared for the real world with interview prep, career counseling, and personal branding. However, there was no preparation for the reality of the nine to five. With no end in sight, I feared, "Is this it?" My need to be someone was eating me alive. I needed to align myself with something greater, something to work on and call my own. I started with stories, unconnected and unsure what the book was going to be about. Inspiration can strike us in unexpected places; for me it was my morning commute. BE SOMEONE was plastered into my mind and I found my thesis in the idea "you need vision to be someone." Then 2020 happened, and with that, the erosion of the one-hundred-year-old dynasty of the nine to five. As of this writing there is no clear solution to the 2020 pandemic, but the consensus is we will get through this, eventually. The digital age has given so much power to the individual; a single person can change the world. The 2020s will be an era of change, and, with this change, an opportunity to be someone.

INTRODUCTION

———

LOST IN THE WOODS

In 1864, a young Scottish American man named John Muir left school in Wisconsin to join his draft-dodging brother in Southern Ontario. This young man had a deep interest in botany, going on hikes in the most rugged of terrains, and how things work.

While he was living in Canada, he explored forests and swamps to study plants. Low on funds and with winter on the way, John decided to take his brother's advice and work at a sawmill. He worked there until it burned down in February of 1866.

In March of 1866, he settled in Indianapolis, Indiana, and got a job working in a wagon wheel factory. His creativity improving machines and processes got him promoted to a supervisor position, earning him $25 a week.

A year later, at the age of twenty-eight, an accident changed his life forever. A tool he was working with slipped and struck his left eye, deeply scratching his cornea. The damage affected his right eye as well, causing him to become blind. He was confined to a dark room for six weeks, with fear that he might never see again.

At the end of six weeks, his sight was restored. Not only could he see again, but he also described this moment as "being able to see the light."

He had an "epiphany," or a moment of sudden and great revelation or realization.

> *"This affliction has driven me to the sweet fields," he said. "God has to nearly kill us sometimes, to teach us lessons."*[1]
>
> -JOHN MUIR

He realized in these literal dark times that at any moment you can lose something that can change your life. Rather than wait for another accident to happen in the workplace, he decided to take a more meaningful approach in his life by doing what he was most interested in, which was exploring the unmapped American wilderness and documenting every step along the way. John walked from Kentucky to Florida, taking the most untamed route, and wrote books about it.

---

1   Amy Marquis Leinbarch, "A Mountain Calling," *National Parks Magazine,* Fall 2007.

In 1871, John wrote his first article for publication, "Yosemite Glaciers," published in the *New York Tribune*. John Muir's work going forward was met with acclaim by both the scientific and artistic communities. Muir focused his efforts on his ultimate vision of preservation and the establishment of national parks.

In the 1880s, John advocated for greater federal preservation, as well as a halt on the destruction of natural resources, especially in the Yosemite region. It was his mission to get the government to establish more national parks, and he fought for the conversion of Yosemite from state park to national park only to be met with fierce opposition from loggers and industrialists looking to ravage the land of its resources.

Nevertheless, in 1890, both Sequoia National Park and Yosemite National Park were established, and later, in 1896, John was appointed advisor to the National Forestry Commission under President Cleveland.

In a 1903 letter, President Roosevelt personally asked Muir to take him on a trip through Yosemite, and Muir accepted. During the four days spent together, John detailed the vast and beautiful natural history of California and the importance of its protection.

Roosevelt was enchanted by this trip, taken with the grand sequoias, native wildlife, and horseback ride to Glacier Point, where he woke up covered in snow. During the rest of Roosevelt's time in office, he set aside 148 million acres of forest reserves and doubled the number of national parks.[2]

THE RACE FOR RIGHTS

In 1972, Harvey Milk left his job with the Great American Insurance Company to move to San Francisco, California, with his partner, Scott Smith. They settled in the Castro district and opened a shop called Castro Camera.

Businesses nearby weren't happy about a gay-owned company in their neighborhood, and there were threats to have the police called on them to shut down their business. In reaction to this hostility, Milk swore to bring together the gay community and their businesses to create areas where they were safe.

In the '70s, there was a large migration of homosexuals— hundreds a week—to San Francisco and the Castro district. Milk made a list of businesses that were friendly to gays. Those that were thrived, and those that weren't didn't.

Recognizing the need for a voice in the gay community, Milk joined the race for city supervisor and became the first openly gay politician in the history of the United States.

He handed out waivers in the streets and shook hands with as many people as he could. "My name is Harvey Milk and I want to recruit you."

---

2   "Remembering John Muir's Legacy on his Birthday," *DOI* (blog), April 21, 2017, accessed on March 5, 2020.

Milk had drifted through life up to this point, but he found his vocation, according to journalist Frances FitzGerald, who called him a "born politician."[3]

Milk had a lot of support from the growing gay community, but he was defeated in the first attempt for city supervisor. Milk saw himself as part of a movement—more than just a candidate—and ran again in 1975.

Again, by just a few votes, he was defeated.

In the years to come, many smalls wins moved the needle for Milk to take office. George Moscone was elected mayor of San Francisco. Moscone recognized that Milk and the gay community had influence on the election, as one to two hundred thousand of the seven hundred and fifty thousand of the city's population were gay. Moscone showed his support for their movement by making Milk a city commissioner.

In 1977, Milk was elected as city supervisor. In the eleven months that he was in office, Milk sponsored a civil rights bill that outlawed discrimination based on sexual orientation and designed a bill to get people to pick up their dog poop (the number-one problem, according to a city-wide poll).

In November 1978, Milk and Mayor Moscone were assassinated by Dan White, who had recently lost his spot as a fellow city supervisor.

---

3 Fitzgerald, Frances, "A Reporter at Large: The Castro – I," *The New Yorker,* July 21, 1986.

Monuments were erected, and streets across the US were named in honor of Milk for his sacrifice to move the LGBTQ+ movement forward.

Anne Kronenberg, his final campaign manager, wrote of him: "What set Harvey apart from you or me was that he was a visionary. He imagined a righteous world inside his head and then he set about to create it for real, for all of us."[4]

From the film MILK (2008)[5]

HAVING VISION

BE SOMEONE is a look at special moments like these, the moment vision takes enough shape to light a path to move forward on. It will help us understand how those from humble beginnings grow to leave legacies that changed their lives and the world, whether it be an entrepreneur leaving their cozy nine-to-five job, a wanderer longing to be an adventurer, or someone fed up with what is considered normal and feeling there is need for change.

The stories of John Muir and Harvey Milk are examples of what it means to be someone. Although their stories may seem unrelated, they both have a common pattern. First, they both had a sense of a greater purpose: what they currently were doing was not satisfying to them, and they felt the need to do something different.

---

4   Leyland Winston, *Out in the Castro: Desire, Promise, Activism* (San Francisco: Winston Leyland, 2001), 37.

5   Van Sant, Gus dir, *MILK*, October 28, 2008.

The feeling of wanting to do more, also known as the need to be someone, but not being quite sure where to put this energy, is something people all over the world ponder. Some people get lucky, or unlucky, and something happens to them to push them into finding their meaning.

The second commonality is the defining moment. For Muir, it was an epiphany brought on by being set in a stage of desperation when he lost his sight for six weeks. For Milk, it was when "enough was enough" when putting up with the homophobic business community and opportunity in the growing gay community of San Francisco. These triggers provided the nudge needed to figure out a vessel to funnel this energy.

In addition to inspiration and epiphanies, these triggers can come from many different places, such as opportunities, tragedies, desperation, and proving others wrong, among other factors. These triggers are not binary; the change comes from mixing different sources, such as inspiration with opportunity, which is what Milk did by mixing the need for change with the opportunity of the growing gay community in San Francisco.

As Marc Randolph, cofounder of Netflix and author of *That Will Never Work*, says, "Epiphanies are rare, and when they appear in origin stories, they are oversimplified or just plain false. We want our Isaac Newton sitting under the apple tree when the apple falls moment. But the truth is usually more complicated than that."[6]

---

6   Marc Randolph, *That Will Never Work* (New York: Hachete Book Group, 2019), 8.

Third, their defining moment leads to the development of a vision. The vision, once fulfilled, is what they are remembered for.

Muir had a vision of conserving the American ecosystem; he did so by publishing over three hundred articles and twelve books and by cofounding the Sierra Club, which helped establish several national parks after he died. Today the club has over 3.8 million members.[7]

Milk campaigned three times, organized labor among gay and immigrant communities to boycott businesses that were not friendly to gay people. and developed key political relationships to realize his vision of equal rights.

The need to be someone, a defining moment, and the pursuit of a vision seem to be mutually common traits for many that have built legacies.

To better understand this concept, I am going to walk you through the lives of entrepreneurs, adventurers, politicians, activists, and artists who have left a lasting impact. The point is to answer a simple question that a lot of people struggle with: *Who do I want to be?*

Who do I want to be, or phrased another way, what does it mean to be someone? This book is for the graduating class of 2020 and beyond.

---

7   "About the Sierra Club," Sierra Club, accessed October 11, 2020.

THE NEED TO BE SOMEONE

In a world that has been turned upside down, what does it mean to be someone in 2020?

We live in an era where this question is not readily answered. We are no longer satisfied with the 1950s version of the "American Dream." Once upon a time, getting a nine-to-five factory job, having a couple of kids, buying a house, and going to your place of worship was satisfying.

In the Rona '20s, the nine-to-five has been replaced by work from home, more couples are waiting to have kids, houses are bought as investments rather than homes, and day by day, more people are losing faith in organized religion.[8][9][10]

As a young professional at the dawn of my career, I have felt lost at times, like I am not contributing to something greater. I have felt like my work doesn't make much of an impact and that later in life I will have no legacy to look back on. Seventy percent of people in the workforce today are unhappy with their job and are looking to make a switch.[11] This book is for that seventy percent.

---

8   Ashley Stahl, "New Study: Millennial Women Are Delaying Having Children Due To Their Careers," *Forbes*, May 1, 2020.

9   Laura Kusisto, "Investors Are Buying More of the U.S. Housing Market Than Ever Before," *Wall Street Journal*, June 6, 2019.

10 "America's changing religious landscapes," Pew Research Center, May 12, 2015.

11 Marcel Schwartes, "A New Study Reveals 70 Percent of Workers Say They Are Actively Looking for a New Job. Here's the Reason in 5 Words," *Inc*, December 18, 2020.

I share stories from my own perspective as a millennial entering the workforce. Since I made the move from my home city of Houston, Texas, to Seattle, Washington, I've been honing my vision to find out for myself what it means to be someone. To understand vision from different perspectives, I interviewed the founders of industry-leading enterprises and members of large social movements.

Fair warning, I am not a PhD candidate, scientist, affluent CEO, or industry executive with years and years of experience. As a representative of this generation, I am, however, a prime subject to gather data on these questions we have about the new generation of workers.

Ever since I entered the workplace, I have been grappling with the thought of "is this it?" I go in depth on my thought process as a sample of the millennial population and how I've come to vision as the solution to reach self-actualization.

Finally, this book is for the leader who wants to understand what it means to *operationalize* vision.

But first, how did we get here?

PART 1

WHAT IT MEANS
TO BE SOMEONE

To define is to limit.

-OSCAR WILDE

CHAPTER 1

A MILLENNIAL'S MALAISE

———

It was 8:15 a.m., Houston, Texas, time. "Well, I am gonna be late, again." I was merging onto I-45 South moving at a molasses pace in bumper-to-bumper traffic.

When I finally snailed my little Hyundai into my desired lane, I saw the iconic "BE SOMEONE" graffiti come into view. The blocky turquoise letters were barely visible from the streams of light coming from the sun rising in the east.

I closely watched the F-150 ahead of me as I pulled out my phone to take a picture of the urban artwork to post to Instagram. Being a connection-starved millennial, it almost seemed like a requirement.

I inched a little bit closer to the F-150, aiming the mural into the center of my screen. Got the pic. Mission accomplished. Dopamine released.

I pulled into the parking garage around 8:30 a.m., right when class started. It was clear I was going to be at least five minutes late, so I went to my trunk and pulled out a can of Coke. My advanced professional selling professor had us sign an agreement that if we were ever late to class, we would buy him a Coke. I kept a twenty-four pack in my trunk for good measure.

I walked in, slapped the Coke on his desk, gave him a quick nod, and headed to the nearest open chair of the thirty-five-seat classroom of MH 365A.

Sauntering past my snickering colleagues, I sunk into my seat and slid my phone out under the desk, staring at my "BE SOMEONE" post that had already garnered five likes. As I sat there, I pondered what the artist meant by "BE SOMEONE."

My first thought as to what it means to be someone is to be recognized by their community for a series of achievements—like an adventurer who puts their name on a piece of land they discover; or a singer who goes on tour and releases albums with millions of adoring fans.

Each persona created their own legacy by doing something that allowed them to BE SOMEONE. Everyone thinks that you have time to build a legacy, but building a legacy is something you must actively work towards.

A NEW START

September 16, 2018. It felt like the last day of summer as I stepped off the plane into Sea-Tac International Airport.

I followed the shared parking signs to Uber and Lyft pickup and waited for Ahmed to pick me up. He scooped me up and we headed downtown.

"Man, living here is crazy expensive. I'm telling you, since you're new here, you should look into renting a room, much cheaper than an apartment."

Ahmed was right: when I called him on Uber to take me from the airport to downtown, the ride alone was a bite out of my already bleeding checking account.

"But man, I love it here, I moved here because I have a sister here; sure, the winters are depressing, but the summers make up for it." Weaving in and out of tall evergreen trees, when we emerged from the forest leading to the city, we saw the Seattle skyline starting to peak over the horizon.

"I came here from Somalia, took me forever to get my papers in order, I hope to be a citizen soon." We drove up the double-decker highway that took us straight into the city. If I had known that the Viaduct was going to be torn down in a few months, I might have taken more pictures.

"Supposedly because it's not earthquake safe, but I heard the wealthy elite wanted to tear it down to increase the waterfront's property value." Sure, it was ugly, but it added to the urban jungle look that downtown had going. Also, there was probably no better way to see the city.

"It will always be my home, but really Somalia is too boring, nice beaches though."

When we pulled onto the corner of Pike and 1st Street in downtown, I caught a vibe from the man playing "Voodoo Child" on his Fender Stratocaster on the sidewalk. I got out in front of the hostel and said my goodbye to Ahmed, thanking him for the ride and the story of his move here.

***

The entrance of the Green Tortoise Hostel contains an ATM and a narrow stairway that leads to the lobby. I scaled the stairs with my two large suitcases in hand, pressing two Brits up against the wall.

I plopped my suitcases by my side and slid my gym bag off my shoulder as I began the check-in process. "Wow, two weeks, eh? That's a pretty long time to stay at a hostel; you're not moving here, right? Cause if you are, you can't stay here."

"Of course not! My next stop after this is Portland," I said through a shit-eating grin.

As the receptionist took my info, she said I should leave one of my suitcases up front with her, as both suitcases would probably not fit in my locker of the eight-person shared room.

The reality was, yes, I had decided to move to Seattle. However, at the time I was so broke that I couldn't afford a hotel in the city, so I settled with the low cost of the of one-star (now two-star) hostel known as the Green Tortoise.

I got an offer with a pretty good company and was given three weeks to relocate from Houston, Texas, to Seattle, Washington. After getting rejected from over fifty companies, I did not want to let this opportunity pass. And at $35 a night and only a ten-minute walk from the office, I couldn't have picked a better spot.

The Green Tortoise had a communal feel to it. The ripped green upholstery in the kitchen area was probably the comfiest place to sit, even more than my bed. They were serving tacos at seven that night on the house; I made sure to add that to my calendar.

The receptionist led me upstairs to my room, swiped a keycard that opened the door, and then handed it to me.

"You're in luck, you got a bottom bunk." There were eight beds in the room, four bunks lined against the left and right side of the room. My bunk laid against the end of the left wall. Between both beds was a window; from the second story, you could hear all the commotion coming from Pike Place Market across the street.

I stuffed my suitcase and bags in the dusty locker underneath my bunk and then crossed the street to explore Pike Place. I could not get over how good the weather felt. No humidity,

72 degrees, it felt nice to be outside. When I got on the plane in Houston, it was 91 degrees but felt like 105 degrees.

Pike Place is a winding labyrinth of diners, antique stores, food vendors, fishmongers, and breweries sandwiched between downtown and the city's waterfront. I waded through a crowd of people and made my way to a bright set of lights that read "Post Alley." I locked eyes with a nearby fruit stand vendor: "Try this! Pear fresh from the San Juan Islands! Guarantee you'll never have a fresher pear!" I threw back the plastic thimble of pear slices he gave me; it tasted like pear.

I melted back into the crowd and squeezed into Post Alley. The alley was full of tourists. I would have stopped to take a picture with the gum wall, but the closer I got to it the more it made want to retch. You could see the saliva glistening from the freshly placed gum pieced together to form a heart.

Around the corner from the gum wall was Pike Place Improv, a theater that specialized in stand-up comedy. I thought about my old dream of being a stand-up comic. Maybe I could check out this place after work and see if they had any open mic nights.

The alley opened into the waterfront. I walked to Pier 66 and scaled the stairway to the top of the world trade center building. From here you could see the top of the space needle, Mount Rainier in the distance, and Smith Tower sticking out like a sore thumb in the city skyline. Cargo ships were loading containers into the port south of downtown. From the way the sunset was hitting the container cranes in the distance, it looked like Star Wars AT-ATs were roaming the Puget Sound.

It was getting late and my first day of work was tomorrow, so I went back to the Green Tortoise for some dinner.

"That's a pretty big move all by yourself, you don't know anyone here?" I was chatting with an older gentleman; I think his name was Mike.

"Not a soul," I said, scooping a mixture of ground beef and lettuce onto half a taco shell.

"Congratulations, that's a big move," said Mike, already a part of the clean plate club. "Do you play chess?"

"I do, actually. Are you trying to get a game in?" I responded, sprinkling some shredded cheese onto my half taco.

"Great, meet me in the smoke room when you're done, they have a board we can play on." Mike stood up from the dinner table and walked to a door with a chalkboard that had "SMOKE ROOM" written on it.

I savored my free tacos and then followed him inside.

***

I jiggled the brass knob; it was barely attached to the door. The door creaked open; Mike was sitting at a table playing against an even older gentleman with a braided beard.

"Pull up a chair, bud, you're next," said Mike.

I dragged a sofa chair from across the room to the small square table. I lowered myself into the chair and could feel the plank from the frame press against my back. I was lower than Mike and our new friend due to the all the fluff in the cushions being worn out.

Three old Asian women were smoking cigarettes at a table under a window. For some reason it wasn't open. They were swiping through their phones, showing off pictures they had taken that day. I later discovered that these three ladies were from China on vacation.

"Checkmate," said Mike, unimpressed. The tall, bearded man sighed, stood up, and walked away.

"What's your name and where you from, bud?"

"My name is Adam and I'm from Texas," I said proudly.

"Okay Adam from Texas, your move."

I moved my pawn and Mike moved his; each move I made had twice as much thought as the last. I am glad we didn't have a chess clock setup.

The tobacco and marijuana smoke clouds kept coming as if someone left on a fog machine. There must have been more smoke than oxygen in that room; the only time smoke ever got out was when someone opened the door, kind of like a sauna.

"I'm sorry Adam, you deserve better than this." Mike took my queen and put me in check. Sometimes you can see the end a few turns in advance, and you can either play it to the end or quit. I'm too stubborn to quit, so I rode the loss out like a champ.

I thanked Mike for the game, shook his hand, and stumbled out of the smoke room.

***

I went back to my room and crashed onto my bed, but I couldn't sleep.

Maybe it was the very lumpy mattress. It could have been my bunkmate, who seemed to be suffering from sleep apnea and snored like a Boeing 747. It could also have been the anxiety of starting my big boy career. It could have been being alone in a new city. Maybe it was a combination of all the above. Regardless, I was in a sleep-deprived thought frenzy.

Why did I leave my comfortable part of the country? I had a friend group, could visit my family whenever I wanted to; now I am here, I am alone.

My bunkmate let out a particularly loud snore, then paused for a moment. I thought maybe I was free from the airfield and could finally rest peacefully, but before I could finish the thought another 747 took off. It's amazing how he didn't wake himself up.

The longer I laid awake, the more my back ached and my mind raced. *You know, I haven't signed a lease anywhere yet. I could just get the next flight home and live with my parents for a while.*

Why did I leave in the first place? Why did I leave in the first place? I was thinking back to the moment when I applied for the job that took me across the country. I filled the entire month of July with interviews for companies in Austin that ended up going nowhere.

I wanted to go somewhere new. I have always had the fear of being in the same place today as the year before. I wanted to chase an opportunity that got me excited. And I got rejected by a bunch of exciting companies near me, so I widened my scope of applications.

I had this *feeling* of wanting to do something great, something challenging and rewarding. Like a project you work on every day, and even after a hard day of work, you wake up the next morning excited to get back at it. Something to constantly build. I want to feel like I'm doing something important. I want to make an impact.

I didn't quite have the vision yet, so I figured it would be best to get some learning in the real world.

As I lay there thinking, I remembered that day back in Houston trying to catch a glimpse of that iconic graffiti.

BE SOMEONE. What does it even mean and why do I know I want to be someone?

I moved here because I want to BE SOMEONE. I have this feeling of wanting to do something great, this sense of purpose to create something. This move was a defining moment for me to nourish this feeling and stimulate the creation of a vision for me to BE SOMEONE.

Not everyone has this feeling. Some people choose to simply have a family and let that be their legacy. There's nothing wrong with that, unless, of course, you have that feeling of wanting to be someone. You don't want to be left with a hollow anxiety of missing out.

I brought this feeling up to a few colleagues before; one of them defined it as an entrepreneurial spirit. The psychologist Victor Frankl famously wrote that searching for meaning is the primary motivational force in man.[12]

We can let this force fill us with fear of the future, or we can use it to find vision to satisfy the need to be someone.

Existentialist psychologists such as Rollo May in particular spoke of the motivation to find

meaning, to make sense of one's existence as a defining feature of humanity, separating it from all other living creatures.

---

12   Viktor Frankl, *Man's Search for Meaning* (Boston: Beacon Press, 2006).

Why do I have this feeling when others don't? Are some people just born with it, or is it passed on from parents? Is it something layered on as we grow up? Why do a lot of us want to be someone while a lot of us just want to belong?

CHAPTER 2

SPIRIT AND VISION

"Everyone seems to have a clear idea of how other people should lead their lives, but none about his or her own."
— **PAULO COELHO,** *THE ALCHEMIST*

GREATER PURPOSE

The rickety old wooden floor creaked under my weight as I walked across the living room. The light from the blaze dimly lit the cracked walls of the aging house. I sat down by the fireplace, stoking the log to get more flame out of it. Despite being the first day of March 2020, it was still quite cold in Seattle.

Things aren't going well at work, I thought.

Being in sales, you make most of your money through commission. My promotion put me on a team exploring the new sales model. I'm still learning the role, but I haven't made much traction yet. I haven't gotten paid commission in three months.

What am I doing? I cannot say that I was too excited for the promotion; it was more of what I was already doing. Same department, different title. Like instead of eating cheese pizza daily, it's now pizza with toppings. It's better, but I've been eating pizza all year. I want steak, or salad, or poke. I want something different. I want to live my dream.

I believe this is what one would call a state of "desperation." The money is no longer coming in, the city I moved to is still lonely after years of moving here, and I am starting to lose passion for my profession. I tell myself I need more experience, to grow up more, and make mistakes on someone else's dime before I take that leap into entrepreneurship. What I truly want, or at least what I think I want.

"Desperation is the final and inevitable result of months or years of accumulated neglect that brings us to that point in time where we find ourselves driven by urgent necessity to find immediate answers to life's accumulated challenges."

-JIM ROHN, AUTHOR OF *THE FIVE MAJOR PIECES TO THE LIFE PUZZLE*

They say you get closer to happiness when your actual self and your perception of yourself become closer together. I have an idea of who I want to be.

If I were being true to myself and heading down the road of my personal legend, I would be bringing the legend back to life. Carrying on my family's legacy of entrepreneurship. Bringing حلويات عرفات {*hallelujaht arafat, a Middle Eastern bakery*} to the United States.

I would be designing the systems, developing the primary aim, the strategic objective, the people strategy, the marketing strategy, defining the organizational structure, and documenting every operation so precisely that the business can be built again and again.

But I don't.

When I think of what is blocking me from pursuing this, the first thing that comes to mind is fear.

Fear of losing my job.

Fear of getting kicked out of my house because I can't pay the bills.

Fear of getting sued.

Fear of getting fined.

Fear of telling someone they must go home because I can't pay their salary.

Fear of not being able to pay back investors or lenders.

Fear of being ostracized by my tiny community.

Fear of failure.

But what I fear most of all is living in a constant state of what if. The fear of being in the same place in one year as I am today. The fear of living a life of mediocrity, one without passionate pursuits, where I am just another brick in the wall.

"Pushing through fear is less frightening than living with the underlying fear that comes from a feeling of helplessness."

-SUSAN JEFFERS, AUTHOR OF *FEEL THE FEAR AND DO IT ANYWAY*

This feeling of helplessness, this desperation, can manifest itself in a different way, too. This feeling that pulls us to do something more—Abraham Maslow classified it as "self-actualization." [13] It is the desire that needs to be satisfied when all the other necessities are satisfied; shelter, food, water, community, love, belonging, satisfying work.

I recognize that as the need to "be someone."

---

13   Abraham Maslow, "A Theory of Human Motivation," *Psychology Review,* 1943. 50, 370-396.

GROWTH MOTIVATION

Maslow believed that at the core of every neurosis was an unfulfilled need. If a person did not have a way to meet their basic needs for safety, belonging, love, and respect, that person would create a neurotic symptom to attempt to satisfy in some way this unmet need. He found that when his patients' needs were met, their neuroses disappeared.[14]

Take a child who comes up with an imaginary friend, for example. A handful of small studies have tried to dig into the psychology of kids with imaginary friends. One study suggested that relationships with invisible beings fulfill a child's need for friendship and are more common among firstborn or only children.[15]

There's something in people motivating them to move beyond their current situations into new understanding and new life that could not be understood as maintenance of homeostasis. He called this motivation "**Growth Motivation**" and used it to explain the tendency of people as they grow.[16]

He saw this **Growth Motivation** as natural and foundational because it was exhibited in children with the joy they found in new discovery, and not only children, but also those individuals who he referred to as "self-actualized," who continued

---

14 Dan Hoffman, "Maslow - Deficiency vs. Growth Motivation," *NO NONSENSE PSYCHOLOGY* (blog), May 8, 2009.

15 Tracy R. Gleason, et al., "Imaginary companions of preschool children," *Psychological Development* Vol 36(4), (Jul 2000): 419-428.

16 Abraham Maslow, *Toward a Psychology of Being* (Eastford: Martino Fine Books, 2011).

to be motivated by the continuous joy of learning, exploring, and growing.[17]

This tendency for growth, he believed, was important to gain an understanding of the functioning of healthy people, as unmet needs were understood to be the seeds of mental illness.

This need for growth helps us understand why we have a need to be someone.

SPIRIT TO FUEL THE VISION

I have discussed the feeling of wanting to do something more many times in the past. It's been defined in many ways: by psychology as self-actualization, in business as the entrepreneurial spirit. Something that needs to be nourished, a feeling within a lot of different people.

This is the feeling that compels us to take risks and move society forward. In economics, the factors of production are land, labor, and capital, and I know some would argue that the fourth factor is entrepreneurship.

In his book *The Lean Startup,* Eric Ries defines entrepreneurship as, "a human institution designed to create new products and services under conditions of extreme uncertainty."[18]

---

17   Dan Hoffman, "Maslow - Deficiency vs. Growth Motivation," *NO NONSENSE PSYCHOLOGY* (blog), May 8, 2009.

18   Eric Ries, *The Lean Startup* (New York: Crown Publishing Group, 2011), 8.

Many think of an entrepreneur as someone who starts businesses. This is true; however, nowadays the definition of entrepreneurship extends far beyond business and economics. At a high level, entrepreneurship is the creation of value.[19]

Entrepreneurship can be applied to build social enterprises as well as business enterprises. In my case, the entrepreneurial spirit burdens me to take business risks and build something new.

Unfortunately, it can't be ignored. To live with it, it needs to be nourished. You can feed it small things at first, like reading books or going to relevant events, but eventually it will want more.

I believe this spirit shares a spot with self-actualization on Maslow's hierarchy of needs. Figuring that out could be the hardest part of living life. There's a reason why there is a whole subject around it in philosophy and psychology.

When one has this feeling, the need for self-actualization or the entrepreneurial spirit, it is hard to satisfy it without a vision.

Whether you want to be a business entrepreneur, author, artist, scientist, journalist, or whatever fill-in-the-blank project, you need to have a vision of what that looks like for

---

19   Johan Gaddefors and Alistair R. Anderson, "Entrepreneurship and context: when entrepreneurship is greater than entrepreneurs," *International Journal of Entrepreneurial Behavior & Research*, Volume 23 Issue 2 (2017).

you. From there you can use the energy from your entrepreneurial spirit to work toward your vision of what it means to be someone.

Finding your vision is not easy. *You need to start with a hypothesis.* Determine who you think you want to be. Learn what satisfies your spirit. If it does, you might be headed in the right direction.

The vision gives your spirit something to be anxious about, somewhere for all this energy to go. What should I be doing right now? Will it help with the overall creation of my vision? If yes, keep moving forward; if no, you need to reevaluate.

To satisfy the spirit, you need to work toward your vision.

Years ago, when I was living in the Middle East, my dad had just started living the vision of Arafat Sweets (it rhymes in Arabic: *Halaluyaht Arafat).* We started with one store in Amman, Jordan. My dad's vision was that of scale: bakeries across the Arab world.

My dad goes by Bill. He adopted this name when he moved to the US, when the local Houstonians wouldn't recognize him as Nabeel. The vision started when he was a young man living in Palestine.

***

FROM HUMBLE BEGINNINGS

It was a hot day in Nablus, Palestine. The mid-1970s were a big time of change for the territory that was recently stripped of its country status. As the dirt met the asphalt, it looked like lava spewing into the sea as it hardened and formed street.

"Man, this Kunafa sucks, I can't believe we spent ten shekels on this crap," said Samir.

Samir wiped his mouth on his wrist. He proceeded to chisel away at the melted cheese that began to fuse with the Styrofoam plate. "Baba always did it better, he knew the right cheese to use, the right amount of oil so it wasn't too greasy; he made his own kunafa topping, I swear nobody could make it the way he could. I wish he was here with us today to make some more."

Bill dipped the last bit of his bread into the mixture of oil and pepper.

The more Zaid and Zaatar you eat, the smarter you will become. Bill heard that from his mother all the time growing up. It was just starting to dawn on him that bread and oil are a lot cheaper than meat.

"Ramadan's coming up, I'm excited and scared at the same time. I can't imagine this will get much easier," Samir said, clapping the flour off his hands.

"Insha-allah, we can do this, each penny saved is for the family," said Bill methodically, looking at the oil drip from his last piece of pita bread.

"Alright, break's over, that concrete ain't gonna pour itself," the supervisor squawked at Bill and Samir. Sweat dripped from Bill's beak, his keffiyeh cooking him like a potato but necessary to keep the sun from roasting his skin.

Bill grabbed his spade and started shoveling and smoothing the concrete. He thought about a time when he didn't have to work, a more vulnerable and innocent time. His father Rasheed would make Kunafa and they would have it every night after dinner during Ramadan. The warm, rich, sweet-and-salty cheese mixed with syrup and pistachio made a whole day of not eating and drinking bearable. The thought of getting that sweet slice of Kunafa got him through the day.

Who doesn't love Kunafa? When done right, there is no resisting it. Bill scraped off a piece of concrete stuck to the toe of his beige rubber work boots. The gloves were protecting his hands from the heat reflected on the shovel, but his hands still blistered by the end of day. At night, he would pick the blisters and bandage them up for the next day of shoveling.

Pouring concrete all day was not fun, but building the road from Nablus to Ramallah did not last forever. Plus, there was more meaning in work that was connecting the country. Most importantly, it paid more than being a dishwasher.

"Worst ten shekels I have ever spent." Samir chucked the plate into the desert like a frisbee. "Pure shit, I can't believe good sweets are so hard to come by."

The mechanical shoveling mixed with heat had Bill's mind racing. *If bad shit sells, how much better would good shit do?*

If my dad were still around and running the sweet shop, it would be the most popular spot in town. People from all over country would come for it—I mean, they would if there were roads connecting the towns. Better yet, any Arab city: if a shop was opened it would be hot.

It was an hour till sunset; around one hundred and fifty meters of road must have been added. "Another day, another inch." Nabeel peeled his gloves off and shoved them in his back pocket. Samir plugged one nostril and blew out a dusty booger.

"I'm clocking in with the boss, I'll meet you at the house; I am going to pick up some Kunafa on the way home."

"I thought it was the worse Kunafa you've ever had?"

"Yeah, but even bad Kunafa is still pretty good."

"Someday, I am going to have stores all over the Arab world, and you will be able to get good Kunafa, and everyone will know what it is and will be able to share it."

"Oh yeah?" Samir remarked doubtfully. "In the meantime, let me have ten shekels so I can bring us home some Kunafa today."

***

The vision started out as an idea. Over the years it was forgotten for a bit but was always brooding in the back of Bill's head. He would go to the US for school and eventually open several different businesses. But the vision was still there. After much learning, eventually the path became clearer, and Arafat Sweets was reborn.

The need to fulfill this vision was carved out for years, not acting upon it until certain opportunities ended, allowing the old vision to come to light again.

The thing about growth motivation is that the more you feed it, the bigger it gets and the more nourishment it requires. Bill had a vision of starting Arafat Sweets, starting with one store in Amman, Jordan. Over time, he built a team that scaled the business to dozens of stores across the Middle East.

The growth mindset seems to be mutual among entrepreneurs, as businesses that remain the same tend to be beat out by those trying their best to grow.

We need vision to satisfy the entrepreneurial spirit. We need vision to realize self-actualization. We need vision to be someone.

CHAPTER 3

THE POWER OF VISION

It was a cold and rainy day in June 2020: not the way I expected the summer to start. We were all gathered in Judkins Park, standing silently in the cold rain.

Not a soul said a word.

The rain was drumming against the hoods of the fellow protesters and their signs. I could feel the cardboard melting in my hands, staining me with black ink. The white acrylic of the words "The Power of the People is Stronger than the People in Power" started peeling in the rain.

We were alerted that the march had started, though we hadn't moved in half an hour. The immense flood of people squeezing onto 23rd created a bottleneck.

As we marched like penguins in the rain of Judkins Park, our slow movement seemed symbolic of the slowly moving steps towards equality. MLK told his "I Have a Dream" speech on August 28, 1963. Although almost sixty years ago, it's become clear that systematic racism targeting African Americans and other minorities is still around in the United States.

On May 25, 2020, the nation was finishing up month three of the lockdown put in place due to the COVID-19 pandemic.

On this day, police officer Derek Chauvin arrested George Floyd when he was trying to use a counterfeit bill. When Floyd was being detained, Chauvin placed his knee on Floyd's neck for eight minutes and forty-six seconds. In the time this was happening, Floyd cried out, "I can't breathe," as three other officers watched.

The footage recorded of the incident was horrifying and shocked the nation so much that protests against police brutality erupted in every major city in the US and across the globe. Movements to "defund the police" and invest in the community were rallying across news media outlets. "ACAB" was spray-painted on the sides of buildings, stop signs, sculptures, and anywhere it could be seen by citizens of the city.

It was reminiscent of Emmett Till, a young African American boy who was brutally murdered after allegedly flirting with Carolyn Bryant Donham, the wife of a white store owner in Jim Crow-era Mississippi. "Nothing that boy did could ever justify what happened to him." Donham (by then seventy-two years old, divorced from Roy Bryant, and twice remarried) admitted she had lied in her court testimony when she said Till had "grabbed her around the waist and uttered obscenities."

Till was kidnapped, beaten, tied to a heavy cotton gin fan, and thrown into a river. His body was so deformed when found that authorities were only able to identify him by the ring on his finger.

Till's mother refused to have him buried immediately and had an open-casket funeral. His funeral was covered by *Jet,* a weekly African-American-run newspaper, and soon over one hundred thousand people viewed his body and heard the horror story of what happened to him.

Outrage over Emmett Till's lynching didn't launch the civil rights movement, which had already begun among African Americans around the country, though it was a large amount of kindling for the movement.

Till's sacrifice had already had an indelible impact on the future of the civil rights movement. On December 5, one hundred days after Till was murdered, Rosa Parks refused to give up her seat on a bus in Montgomery, Alabama. As Parks later said of her actions that day, "I thought of Emmett Till, and when the bus driver ordered me to move to the back, I just couldn't move." Her arrest, of course, sparked the now-famous Montgomery bus boycott that turned the struggle for civil rights into a mass movement led by the then-twenty-six-year-old minister Rev. Martin Luther King Jr.

The nation, kept under lockdown, had immense pressure building up with the killings of Ahmaud Arbery while jogging and Breonna Taylor when she was sleeping in her own house.

With the display of George Floyd's killing by a police officer by pressing his knee on his neck for eight minutes and forty-six seconds, it was the spark that blew the lid off a quarantined nation. The streets were filled with rioting protesters carrying signs that read the names of those who've been forgotten by the justice system: *"Tamir Rice, Emmett Till, Philando Castile, Trayvon Martin; say their names," "defund the police," "think how many WEREN'T recorded."*

All seeking one thing: change.

Martin Luther King's vision of the elimination of systematic racism in the United States and the rest of the world hasn't been fully realized yet, but if we can share in his vision of a place where "we will be judged not by the color of our skin but by the content of our character," we can get there together.

This shift in environment has opened up the opportunity for change yet again: we have a clearer view of the problem than ever, and the position we are in can be the leverage we need to make a huge dent in the root of the problem.

Already, Seattle, Washington, and Austin, Texas, have voted to reorganize their police budget to be invested in community and social services. It is unclear at this point if defunding the police and reinvesting in the community will solve the racial profiling and control the variables where crime is formed, but now we have two test cities to see if defunding the police is an effective solution.

***

Little by little, the crowd of thousands of people finally started to move. Two steps every five minutes. Then three steps. Soon we started setting a pace and went into a march on 23rd street.

Stopping at lights, the black cardboard in my hands was dissolving into mushy ink, coloring my hands and my clothes, dripping onto my forehead as I held it up above my head. The cold rain numbing my hands, it was as if God was testing our merit to see how far we were willing to go.

The cold rain and the crowd of people surely made it a place where we could easily spread the coronavirus.

But we all knew the risks of going out, that we could all be potentially expanding the lifespan of this virus. But as the signs held by the protesters around me read, "Racism is a virus," and it's been going on for years.

Unfortunately, it can't be ended by social distancing. It needs a powerful antidote. An antidote from the people. A change at our core. We all share the vision that Martin Luther King Jr. had back in the 1960s. At this unique point in history where the people are enabled to create change, we might finally take a meaningful step toward the realization of this vision.

VISION APPLIED

When you have a strong, clearly defined vision, the work to get there is less of a grind because every bit of effort goes towards a greater purpose. A vision can not only motivate yourself to get work done in the name of realizing that vision, but also a powerful vision, when told in a compelling story, can influence others to join your cause as well, as in the case of the Black Lives Matter movement.

From social movements to business, we saw this in the innovative era of the '70s and '80s in the founding of today's legacy tech giants. In 1977, Rob Campbell was a young programmer who was excited about the emerging class of personal computers. He began searching for a position at one of the companies at the forefront of the revolution.[20]

Campbell first visited Tandy Computers. "What is your vision for the personal computer?" he asked.

"We think it could be the next big thing on everyone's wish list for the holiday season!" Tandy executives exclaimed.

Uninspired, Campbell visited Commodore, a company that introduced a personal computer in 1977. Commodore's stock was trading at less than one dollar a share. "What is your vision for the personal computer?" Campbell asked.

"We think it could help our stock rise above two dollars a share," Commodore executives said excitedly.

Once again uninspired, Campbell decided to take Steve Jobs up on an invitation to meet for lunch.

---

20 Carmine Gallo, "Steve Jobs and the Power of Vision," *Forbes*, January 18, 2011.

"What is your vision for the personal computer?" Campbell asked Jobs. Campbell said what happened next still gives him goose bumps.

"Steve Jobs was a magical storyteller; for the next hour, he talked about how personal computers were going to change the world. He painted a picture of how it would change everything about the way we worked, educated our children, and entertained ourselves. You couldn't help but buy in."

Vision, said Campbell, was the one thing that separated Steve Jobs from the others.

When searching for a job, at times it can be hard to shop around for companies and not stick with the first company that hands out an offer. But if you can stick out the uncertainty and get in with an organization that you can share your vision with, the reward of being at a company where you can feel fulfilled and contribute to something greater is something not many in the workforce today can share.

In fact, the vast majority of seventeen thousand US workers in nineteen industries who participated in a survey conducted by the nonprofit group Mental Health America and the Faas Foundation said they are unhappy with their jobs. They are so unhappy that seventy-one percent also said they are looking to change employers.[21]

---

21   Gene Marks, "Study: 71 percent of employees are looking for new jobs," *The Washington Post*, October 19, 2017.

Arnold Schwarzenegger, in his message to the class of 2020, said that if he could give one piece of advice to those entering the workforce for the first time, it would be for them to develop their vision.[22]

> *"If you have a vision, then it's not a grind to work towards it. This is why people ask me all the time, Arnold, we saw you in Pumping Iron. You are smiling and looking very happy. The other guys have serious faces and look very intense. I smiled because I was happy to work out. I smiled because I was looking forward to every five-hundred-pound squat, every seven-hundred-pound deadlift, every crunch, every chin up, every curl. Every rep brought me one step closer to the vision of becoming Mr. Universe, the greatest bodybuilder of all time."*

You must have a very clear vision and you must develop that vision.

Ask yourself, "Who do you want to be?" Not what, but who. A disaster can change what you are. It can steal your job and force you inside. But it is who you are that rises in the face of adversity.

---

22 Arnold Schwarzenegger, "My advice to graduates on overcoming obstacles during coronavirus," Instagram Video, May 17, 2020.

"What stands in the way becomes the way."

MARCUS AURELIUS, ONE OF THE GREATEST
MINDS AMONG THE ROMAN EMPERORS.

Life will always be about obstacles in front of you, and it is the way to overcome those obstacles.

When you know your vision, every setback, every stepping-stone, every struggle, all resistance builds your inner strength, builds your character, makes you stronger as a person.

Your mind is no different than your body. You could be doing curls with no weights all day long and nothing would happen to your arm.

But as soon as you put weight into your hand and there is resistance, the bicep will grow and the arm will get stronger.

The same is true with the mind. Embrace the climb towards your vision, and not just the selfie you take at the top. Because the climb is what makes you grow and builds who you want to be.

You can ask any mountain climber that has climbed Mount Everest: they would tell you that it was the climb up to the top that was the learning experience; it was the thing they will remember.

Look back at 2020. Losing your job, staying inside, canceling weddings, canceling travel and other life events to keep the world safe, then the horror that the whole world witnessed with the death of George Floyd.

If there's one thing to take away from this year, it's the challenge. People and society grow when we are challenged, and we stagnate when we are not. 2020 has been an enormous challenge.

The 2020s will be a decade of change socially, economically, and technologically. In strategy, shifting environments can reveal new opportunities. Whether you are trying to start a business or make an impact, having vision will allow you to navigate the changing landscape.

How can we find our vision? A vision can come from many different places, inspiration, desperation, opportunities, and even tragedies. The most proactive way, and hopefully the way most encounter their vision, is from moments of inspiration.

PART 2

CULTIVATING YOUR VISION

Those who see the troubles of others forget their own troubles.
OLD ARABIC PROVERB

CHAPTER 4

INSPIRATION

ARAFAT SWEETS

My dad is one of my biggest inspirations.

He moved to Houston, Texas, from Nablus, Palestine, when he was twenty-six and had almost no money.

He started taking ESL (English as a second language) classes during the day and would valet cars at night. He eventually worked his way into the University of Houston and got his degree in public administration.

Upon graduation, he spent one week as a life insurance agent before he said, "F*** this," and pursued his first business venture.

His friend introduced him to someone who was looking to sell his video rental store (this was the '80s).

The man wanted $60K for the store, but my dad didn't have $60K. He barely had $10K.

"Look bro, I'm not going to lie to you. I don't have $60K, so let's do this. I'll put down fifteen percent and pay the rest over the course of the next two years," said my dad in a very choppy, Arabic-drawn accent mixed with the slang he picked up from living in Sharpstown, a working-class suburb of Houston.

"Make it 1.5 years and you've got yourself a deal," said the store owner.

They shook on this, and eventually my dad would go onto shake the hands of US presidents and world leaders.

In addition to this, he has opened hundreds of businesses in Houston and the Middle East, creating thousands of jobs for locals and immigrants like him.

Between his busy day to day and keeping our current businesses afloat during COVID-19, I managed to snag some time with him to discuss the building of Arafat Sweets.

In 1912 two brothers, Mohammad and Ahmad, and their mother went from Gaza, Palestine, to Beri Al Saba in the Negev Desert with only a tent and a dream at the start of World War I. They set up a makeshift restaurant where Turkish soldiers would eat. Some would pay and some wouldn't.

That store moved to Nablus in the '50s and became a hot spot for many travelers between Jordan and Israel. The store's reputation continued to spread into the early 2000s.

"Our store in Nablus was very popular; people would come from Israel and Jordan to take the sweets back home with them. They would always ask, 'Why don't you open a store in Jordan?'"

A location in Amman, Jordan, made sense. It didn't have the freedom of movement limitations in place by Israel that Palestine was experiencing. There was no room for growth in Palestine, but in Jordan there was.

Jordan is known as the "gateway country" in the Arab world due to its location. It is bordered by Saudi Arabia to the south and the east, Iraq to the northeast, Syria to the north, and Israel and Palestine to the west, strategically located at the crossroads of Africa, Asia, and Europe.

They had a good product that customers loved and a brand that most Arabs recognized.

The opportunity became clear, so Bill wired $40,000 to his brother Mohamed, who was living in Amman at the time, so he could rent a space and buy the equipment.

"It was an immediate success. The first store in Amman was so hot, we had a grand opening that turned into a big party. Famous people would show up, and even the Mayor of Nablus showed up."

◆

My family was living in Houston, Texas, in the '90s and early 2000s. In the summer of 2004, we flew to Jordan as part of a "family vacation" that doubled as a business trip to see firsthand the success of Arafat Sweets.

"The business was doing very well; everybody was talking about Arafat Sweets. That was when I decided to take you and the rest of the kids to Amman, Jordan, to expand," said Bill.

I remember these days. What I didn't know was when we went back to Jordan in the summer of 2005, we were moving there.

I remember packing up all our stuff from our house in the Alief district of Houston. I remember thinking we were going to come back at the end of summer to buy a new house.

I remember my mom breaking the news to me that we were staying. I remember blowing up my PS2 because I didn't have the proper 120-volt to 240-volt adapter.

Tough times.

Especially as a kid who lived his whole life in the United States up to that point. I treasure these times now, as I believe I gained a unique perspective on how others live outside a Western nation.

I did not appreciate it at the time, however.

"When we moved to Jordan, I had my cousin Hasan find us a factory in Sweileh," explained Bill.

I remember Sweileh very well.

Sweileh was a very old area of Amman. It was filled with jagged streets containing butchers, small clothing outlets, small toy stores, and some malls.

I recall I was walking with my mom and my sister when we happened to pass by a butcher. They would hang all the meat outside the store to let us know it was halal, or meat prepared as prescribed by Muslim law.

The string they used to secure the meat must've been old, because as fate would have it, a goat head dangling in the wind snapped and landed in front of my sister.

This might have traumatized my sister, but my mother and I found it hilarious. We still laugh about it to this day.

"Our name was so hot, we were opening one to two stores every month. We had twenty-eight stores in Amman alone. Each store we opened we had a grand opening party."

I remember these parties vividly. My dad would always disappear somewhere with these suited Arabs to discuss business while my siblings and I would try to find some kids who spoke English.

"Other Arab businessman would come from all over the Middle East and ask us to open stores in their country. We started with a factory in Cairo, Egypt," said Bill.

We stayed in Cairo for about two weeks. Cairo is a sprawling metropolis of brown towers and crowds of people. I remember checking out the pyramids of Giza. The stench of the tombs lingered as if the decaying mummies were still there.

"Jeddah, Saudi Arabia, Tripoli, Libya, Dubai, UAE, Bahrain, Qatar, we had forty-eight stores across the Middle East with seven hundred and fifty employees," said Bill.

We were flying. Business was good and we had cash to spare.

"I learned from the United States of America to advertise. I spent $3 million on advertising to let everyone know where to get the best sweets in the Middle East," said Bill.

We did not just spend money with advertising firms. I remember we had a Mercedes that was wrapped in Kunafa vinyl.

When I was in the sixth grade, my Dad would sometimes pick me up in it. I was so embarrassed. Imagine if your parents or guardian picked you up in a pie or burger-wrapped car.

If I had the mindset back then that I have now, I would have been so proud.

"We did well. I was sending pallets of sweets to the US: Los Angeles, Houston, New York, and Dearborn, Michigan. I was in the process of setting up some deals with Sam's Wholesale and Walmart," said Bill.

Dearborn, Michigan, has the highest population of Muslims in the US.

"We almost went public on the Jordanian Stock Exchange; I was going to sell half of the company to an investor for $10 million and get even bigger," said Bill.

I questioned my Dad as to why we never went public or expanded into the US, even though I already knew the answer.

"I got very sick with a stomach bug; I was sick for a year and a half. But what really made me give it up and have us come back to the US was you. You and the rest of our family."

Ever since we moved to Jordan in May of 2005, my family was homesick. Genetically we are half Arab, but in our hearts we are mostly American.

When I got the news we were moving back to the US, I was so excited. The world changed a lot from 2005 to 2008. When we came back, the American economy entered a recession.

Everyone was closing shop. It was a terrible time to start a business, some would say. But one man's failure is another's opportunity.

When we arrived back home to Houston, Texas, we settled in the energy corridor. A laundromat that just shut down had incredibly low rent. Its prime real estate on Westheimer Road gave my Dad an idea.

We locked down an agreement, got six months free rent, and converted it into a car stereo shop. It's still there to this day.

"I've been in the car stereo business for thirty years. I know it even better than sweets!" my dad said excitedly before he had to go.

We have a few car-stereo shops in Houston today, although we had to shut some of them down due to COVID-19, unfortunately. We still have a few bakeries overseas; they are managed by other members of the Arafat family.

IT STARTED WITH A SIP

"Whoa, I threw my head back and my eyes shot wide open. Even from a single sip, I could tell it was stronger than any coffee that I had ever tasted. Seeing my reaction, the Starbucks people laughed."

"Is it too much for you?"

"I shook my head. Then I took another sip. This time I could taste more of the full flavor on my tongue. By the third sip I was hooked."

-FROM HOWARD SCHULTZ'S *POUR YOUR HEART INTO IT*

A lot of people don't know this, but Starbucks did not always sell coffee drinks.

When it was founded in a tiny little outlet in Seattle's Pike Place market, it sold only coffee beans. The market for gourmet coffee was seen as a niche service for coffee connoisseurs. Jerry Baldwin, Gordon Bowker, and Zev Siegel founded the first Starbucks store in 1971, largely based off

Alfred Pete's concept of Peet's Coffee in the Bay Area at the time.

The business model was to sell the finest quality of coffee beans and equipment, a true coffee store. Not a cafe that sold cappuccinos and espressos.

In the late '70s, Howard Schultz started at an entry-level sales role at Xerox, setting up meetings and eventually working his way up to a full-time sales rep. Closing deals, he was making good money. He had done well so far and was satisfied with his work... for a while. "By 1979, though, I was restless in my job. I needed something more challenging."

He heard from a friend that a Swedish company, Perstorp, was setting up a US division for its Hammarplast houseware subsidiary. They put him in North Carolina selling building supplies. After ten months of being away from his wife and his home, New York, he threatened to quit. He must have been one hell of an employee because they moved him back to New York and additionally made him a vice president and general manager, managing twenty sales reps. He was killing it.

"I did that for three years and loved it." Making $75,000 a year with benefits, he had made huge progress for only being out of school for six years. "The life I was leading was beyond my parents' best dreams for me. So no one—especially my parents—could understand why I was getting antsy. But I sensed that something was missing. I wanted to be in charge of my own destiny. It may be a weakness in me: I'm always wondering what I'll do next. Enough is never enough."

Though climbing through the ranks and doing well for himself, living a life the average person would be jealous of, he wanted more. He felt as though he had a greater purpose. This ambition that he had was tipped over into an entrepreneurial endeavor when he checked on a customer that was ordering an unusually high amount of plastic cone filters.

In 1981, Schultz visited Seattle and Starbucks. He visited the stores, their roasting plant, and met Jerry Baldwin and Gordon Bowker. They told him about the origins of Starbucks: how it manifested out of their love for coffee and how they wanted Seattle to have the very best.

Super impressed with Starbucks and sniffing a potential opportunity to be something bigger, Schultz took many trips to Seattle that year, finding every excuse to visit and build the relationship with Baldwin and Bowker.

Finally, he was invited to dinner with their silent investor. It was awkward at first, but they warmed up to each other and were soon conversing as if longtime friends. His friends in New York fell in love with the samples that he brought them, and he explained his hypothesis that cities across the US would love them as well. He proposed working for them in sales, marketing, and merchandising. Schultz spent the next night anxiously awaiting their phone call.

Initially he was rejected for the role, but he did not take no for an answer. "It took me a year to convince Jerry Baldwin to hire me."

They were nervous of the new ideas and the youthful energy that he brought with him. After selling the owners his vision that everyone in America deserved a gourmet coffee experience, they gave in.

In 1982, at the age of twenty-nine, Schultz was hired as their director of retail operations and marketing. At this point Starbucks began providing coffee to fine restaurants and espresso bars.

In 1983, Starbucks sent Schultz to a coffee convention in Milan. While there, he was amazed by the espresso bar culture. On every city block, there was an espresso bar bustling with customers who all had a good relationship with the barista and each other.

Schultz recognized the United States was missing something like this.

Not just a place to get good coffee, but a place to share with other people and exchange ideas. Also known as a "good place" or a "third place:" something that was huge in Europe but virtually nonexistent in the US. Sensing a huge opportunity, he went back to the US excited and hastily told Bowker and Baldwin.

Concerned that Schultz was moving away from the company's mission, they turned down his idea.

Schultz pleaded and persuaded them to see the opportunity the same way he saw it. Not super thrilled about it, they decided to let one store test pilot. They gave him three hundred square feet of the store with an espresso machine. Not much room to work out of, but it was enough to provide him with a proof of concept. The coffee drinks were a huge hit, with lines out the door on most days. People loved Starbucks coffee.

Despite this immense opportunity, the founders still did not want to pivot the main vision of their company. Frustrated, Schultz left Starbucks and founded Il Giornale, a cafe that sold espresso-based coffee drinks.

He faced overwhelming obstacles, such as raising capital as a retail beverage business when all seed money was much more interested in knowledge-based technology companies.

Despite the odds, he attracted the capital needed and opened the first store. Two years later, Bowker and Baldwin sold Starbucks to Il Giornale. Il Giornale assumed the name of Starbucks, and the rest is history.[23]

Schultz had potential, and he knew he wanted to do more. All it took was one sip of a gourmet dark roast coffee to get on board. He had found the inspiration he was looking for.

The inspiration moved him to drop his cozy sales manager career and move across the country to feed his entrepreneurial spirit. When this inspiration met the opportunity

---

23   Howard Schultz, *Pour Your Heart into It* (New York: Hachette Books, 1999).

of the third place, the vision of the modern-day Starbucks began to form.

Schultz saw a chance to be someone. He understood the potential and had his own vision for the company. Rather than step down when his idea was rejected by the Starbucks owners, he went out on his own and started the company he envisioned would sweep the nation.

Schultz's experience with Starbucks teaches us a valuable lesson. If something feels missing in our lives, it's in our best interest to seek out inspiration to fill that void.

2 BROTHERS

The legacy of Arafat Sweets lights a fire in my belly.

As mentioned earlier, lack of resources, expertise, credibility, (and after this was initially written, COVID-19) but above all else fear has blocked me from moving forward on this goal.

But one night, on January 17, 2020, enough was enough.

I finally decided to put my money where my mouth is and put up the filing fee to found 2 Brothers Bakery LLC in Washington state. I changed the name from Arafat because I felt that the word "fat" with a sweet business may not resonate well with an American audience.

I chose the name 2 Brothers because I have a brother. He is not involved directly, but one of my motivating factors is to be a beacon of inspiration for him as well as my entire family to pursue their goals.

From the two brothers in Gaza who had a dream, to the two brothers today who have another dream, our ancestors inspire us to rebuild a legacy in our own way so that we, too, can be someone.

WHEN INSPIRATION IS MOST POWERFUL

It can be difficult to search for inspiration: often, you are not entirely sure what you are looking for.

Inspiration is the most ideal way to find change and purpose and work toward developing a vision. There are other places this change can come from, often from a dark place where it can be very hard to proactively seek out change.

In Schultz's case, inspiration came at a time when things weren't bad. In fact, they were going well in terms of career advancement.

Inspiration is most powerful when we are in a dark place. A wise monk once said, "A single flame can extinguish one thousand years of darkness." A little bit of inspiration can go a long way.

There are times in our life when we think we have a pretty good idea of our vision of who we want to be.

But when things fall apart, our vision can get left behind and we can get stuck in the day to day—where we aren't working toward our vision because maybe we failed in the past and think our vision was too unrealistic to begin with.

Fortunately, we have figures in society who have demonstrated you can always come back to your vision despite setbacks. All it takes is a little spark of inspiration to reignite the fire of your vision.

CHAPTER 5

CREATING OPPORTUNITY

—————

On our way up the 5 into San Francisco, we pulled into the city at around 10:00 p.m. I never had been to this city before; the cold rainy weather that greeted us contrasted against the warm sunny weather of LA.

We drove past offices of notable tech companies: Apple, Google, Facebook, and some lesser-known ones like Evernote and Shutterstock.

All these innovative tech companies, spawned by intelligent visionaries, inspire and educate those they hire and train until they disseminate into organizations of their own when they observe some opportunity to get on board with something bigger. Or so the story goes in Silicon Valley.

It was my final year of university, last spring break, and I was feeling hollow. Like something was missing. Perhaps it was the unease of getting out of school and looking within myself knowing that I hadn't clearly formed my vision yet. I wanted to take my brother with me on this trip to California to inspire myself and get away from the reality of transitioning into the career realm. San Francisco seemed like the perfect place to find it.

I wanted some advice from one of my friends who had moved to Sunnyvale, and I thought I could kill a couple of different birds with one stone taking this road trip out to Cali. He was a Buddhist monk, automatically making him qualified to give life advice.

I reached out to a couple of technology executives on LinkedIn to see if I could get an inside look at the minds that start an industry-changing company and maybe a tour of an office on my spring break. But it wasn't until I was well into my professional career that I was able to meet the mind behind the company that gave me my start.

EVEN IF IT FAILS, THERE IS SOMETHING TO BE LEARNED.

Not all visions are built in a day. Visions from many of today's leading companies are built from the ashes of failed endeavors. Though there isn't much tangibles to take away from a failed venture, there are some intangibles.

One intangible is learning. From any failure, whether it is in business or in life, you can always come out ahead from learning from your experience. These valuable lessons can go forward into powerful visions that can change the world. In the case of Tom Gonser, he changed the way that the world does business.

I reached out to Tom, and we set up a call over the phone at the beginning of the pandemic.

In 1990, Tom moved back from the South Bay Area to Seattle, Washington, to join Craig McCaw to build the wireless data business. Tom was in the middle of a successful career with Apple, closing Macintosh sales and building relationships with K-12 and higher education institutions.

Using his experience from Apple, he moved over to McCaw Cellular, where he oversaw distribution-channel development and strategic partnerships.

"I watched what Craig McCaw was doing and saw the difference between someone who works someplace and someone who does something new. It struck me as there's no reason why I can't do what Craig McCaw does; it's just most people are afraid to try."

In 1985, when Tom graduated from the University of Washington, he worked at Boeing for less than a year. The inertia of a large company like Boeing didn't provide the career path he was looking for: it was too slow.

When companies, governments, and groups grow large, they experience inertia. When they reach a certain size, decisions are made slower, bureaucracy settles in, and adapting to changes in environment takes longer. See the United States government for a relevant example.

After leaving Boeing, Tom searched endlessly for a more dynamic company, which ultimately led him to Apple and then Craig McCaw. However, AT&T's involvement stalled Tom's dynamic growth, so he decided to do something about it.

"We started our own company, and nine months later, with about $180,000 of my own money, it didn't work."

A failure can seem like a big waste of time and resources, and on paper, it is. There's nothing to show for when your company fails. However, there is an opportunity to have valuable learning take place that can steer you away from making those mistakes again.

Needing money, Tom got involved with some more tech start-ups. "Tech start-ups were starting to be a thing, but they weren't—it still wasn't mainstream yet. Sand Hill Road was not a place anyone really heard of."

Sand Hill is a road that runs through Palo Alto, Menlo Park, and Stanford and is well known for its many venture capitalists, notably Kleiner Perkins and Sequoia Capital. Some consider Sand Hill Road the "Wall Street of the West."

In 1994, he moved east and worked at a few more start-ups in Boston—one being Wildfire Communications, which developed a personal electronic assistant that lived in your phone. Many consider Wildfire the precursor to Siri.

Tom learned some things from the failure of his first venture. Combined with his experience of the early stage start-ups, he had a better understanding of what didn't work. More experienced and wary of the pitfalls of the start-up world, he kept his eye out for opportunities. Eventually, one uncovered itself under his own roof.

"My wife is in the mortgage business; she was constantly on the phone talking to borrowers who were wondering what the status of their loan was. I thought, why isn't there a website where you could publish the status of your loan and each person involved could go online, see what's going on, ask questions and submit documents, etc., all electronically."

That's when he came up with the concept of NetUPDATE.

The web in 1998 was not being used for applications; it was primarily marketing. NetUPDATE was about taking a process like mortgage and building an application where people collaborate around the transaction.

"We ended up going from zero to about $35 million value in about a year. We bought the third-largest loan origination software company, which is bizarre, because we're a tech company; they were an established company with thirty thousand customers with real business. But it was a time when you could do that."

Before the dot-com bubble of 2000 burst, internet start-ups grew very quickly. They were being valued on what they could be worth rather than what they were actually worth. Many of these application-based companies had millions of users but no way to generate revenue from them yet. When these hyper-growth companies were unable to pay back their investors, they crashed. A lot of them crashed, and this caused a ripple effect throughout the economy, putting over eight-five thousand people in this field out of work.[24]

Tom was working on getting NetUPDATE acquired; it would have been a zero to $100 million exit in 2.5 years, but that never happened because the market crashed.

"At that point it's like wow, I thought I knew all the things that could go wrong. I couldn't control whether the market collapsed or not, but that's still another thing you need to be cognizant of. At that point I was well stuck into the mode of: *This is what I know how to do, start new things.*"

After the acquisition of NetUPDATE fell apart, he identified what he was good at: making ideas come to life. This realization came from successfully getting NetUPDATE off the ground, confirming his hypothesis with DocuSign, and later ventures that he started. He lives this purpose everyday by working as venture capitalist, helping other entrepreneurs bring their ideas to life.

When you form your vision, it may take some time to realize that it's truly your vision. Tom had it in his mind that he was getting pretty good at bringing ideas to life. His hypothesis was confirmed with the success of NetUPDATE.

Tom had a theory that snail mail wasn't going to be the vehicle delivering agreements over the next thirty years, whether

---

24 Amar Mann and Tony Nunes, "After the Dot-Com Bubble: Silicon Valley High-Tech Employment and Wages in 2001 and 2008." *U.S. BUREAU OF LABOR STATISTICS,* August 2009.

they were $10 or $10 million. The idea of e-signature was floating around the tech world, but everyone was doing it wrong, and there was an opportunity to do it right.

The software originally acquired was too old and did not meet customers' strict security guidelines. Tom and his team needed a way to authenticate the signers' identities for it to be legally binding. When they nailed down digital certificates, customers started listening.

Digital certificates show the signer's IP address and prove the signer is who they say they are. One of the challenges of early adoption after Congress passed the E-SIGN Act of 2000 was that companies were afraid of opening them up to risk when one couldn't validate the identity of a signer.

Once compliance was in place, interviews with customers revealed that what they cared about most was making it a simple process for their customers and people. They also wanted it to integrate with their existing system.[25]

Once these needs were met, DocuSign was ready for launch. DocuSign started in real estate, slowly becoming the industry leader. Coming to the office and being near a fax or a printer was a big hassle for home buyers. Being able to sign from a computer was not only a convenient way to sign agreements, but it also drastically cut down the time to close a deal.

---

25 "The History of Innovation Agreements," *DocuSign* (blog), January 31, 2018, accessed October 12, 2020.

After conquering real estate, DocuSign sought to be the leader in financial services. Then healthcare, education, the public sector, and soon every company in the world was capable of being a customer, every department had a use case, and every person on earth could be a user.

Tom made a lot of the mistakes earlier in his career that were really helpful: going through the process with DocuSign was a lot smoother because the mistakes that could have been made were already experienced, recognized, and avoided.

"I actually think I'm only good for one thing anymore: that's taking an idea that needs to be done and making it happen."

Failing to learn, identifying opportunities, and discovering what you're best at is how Tom Gonser actively built his legacy and left an impact on the world. DocuSign has saved millions of trees through companies not using paper to get their agreements signed. Tom has not only left an impact on the technology community, but on the whole world as well, and for that we remember him.

***

CATCHING UP WITH AN OLD FRIEND
We arranged to meet at the Sunnyvale Zen Center, where my friend was one of the Shifus, or masters of the monastery. The construction of Apple's new building across the street roared as we pulled into the parking lot. The front door was adorned with sticky notes forming a lotus.

When we entered the lobby we were greeted by the receptionist, who went to retrieve Lala for us. When we finally reconnected, we bowed and said "amitofo," (the way Buddhists greet each other) followed by an untraditional hug.

I first met Jian-Tsan when we were both in a psychology class at the University of Houston. He was doing his thesis on the effects of meditation on the mind. I was curious and wanted to learn more, and he told me about the Chung Tai Zen Center of Houston and the meditation classes they offered. As I took those classes, Jian-Tsan moved to Puli, Taiwan, to work at the main Chung Tai monastery.

Upon completion of the meditation classes, the Houston Chung Tai chapter announced their annual pilgrimage to Taiwan to visit the monasteries across the small country. It was my chance to see Lala again and get out of the country for the first time in about ten years, so I tagged along.

He gave us a quick tour of the facility and then led us into the dining hall. We sat on the dark brown wooden floor on a cushioned pad as they laid out a buffet of vegan dishes. Fried tofu, lotus root, white rice, yakisobe, all the fixings you would find in a traditional Chung-Tai Zen Buddhist meal.

My brother, being a carnivorous individual, was less than enthusiastic about the vegan options. When they brought the tea out to conclude the meal, my brother took a walk as I began to probe Jian-Tsan's brain.

I laid out the whole deal of being uncertain of the future, not having a clear vision, and some other things onto him. His response was appropriate, I suppose.

"Dude, just chill out man, that's the best advice I can offer."

"I guess you're right," I said as I slouched over my tea.

"Of course I am; now, I need your help with something. When we moved into this building there was a big patch of dirt left here. We turned that patch into a garden to grow vegetables that we could then serve to our members. Unfortunately, the garden is full of bitter melons now. Bitter melon is an invasive species; they blew up and we have so many that we will be eating bitter melon for weeks."

"Why not just throw the bitter melon out?" I asked, wondering why this solution wasn't obvious.

"We can't waste any of our food here; it's against our tradition: you know we even rinse out our bowls with warm water, not even wasting the sauce or oil left over from the meal."

"What about donating them to a food bank?"

"We looked into that: they can't take this much produce as it perishes too quickly, plus that wouldn't solve the problem of them taking over the garden."

"Sounds like a lot of work to get rid of 'em all; you'll need to get every last single one of them and gather their seeds so they don't sprout more."

"Precisely, but the bigger lesson is to not plant bitter melon seeds in the first place: by their nature they are very bitter; I can see you are not the biggest fan of them either." Jian-Tsan gestured at my unfinished bowl of veggies, which was comprised mainly of the chunky green bits of bitter melon. It made sense why they were trying to get rid of them: it was not very appealing.

"If you want to grow sweet melons, plant sweet melon seeds. If you plant bitter melon seeds, don't expect to harvest sweet melons."

"Okay..." I said, expecting there to be more.

"Are you picking up what I am putting down?"

"I think so: what you're saying is y'all should've never planted bitter melon seeds in the first place."

"That's exactly what I am saying, do you see how that can help you in your situation?"

"Maybe not right now, but when I start a garden, I'll be sure not to plant any bitter melon."

"Think of your own garden and what you want in it," Jian-Tsan said after finishing his tea. "If you want to have a strong harvest in the fall, you need to plant the right seeds today."

"I think I get what you are saying, Lala."

"Good, glad I was able to be of some assistance... Where'd your brother go?" said Jian-Tsan, slightly concerned.

"It's been about half an hour; he's probably bored out of his mind." I rose from the low table and Jian-Tsan escorted me to the lobby.

"Until our paths cross again." We bowed to each other and said one last amitofo before I rejoined my brother at the car.

"Bout time, so where we to next? Lombardi Street? Crissy Field? OH! Can we see Golden Gate Bridge?" said my brother as he slid off the hood of our rental car.

***

In order to get the opportunities we want in the future, we need to plant the seeds of opportunity today. I believe that is the point Jian-Tsan was trying to make. When Tom took the risk of starting his first venture, he failed and lost some money, but that seed he initially planted still grew into something. It didn't grow into a booming business, but it sprouted valuable knowledge that was later used to build incredibly successful companies.

In a way you could say that the death of the first plant was composted and used to fertilize the garden, which, when combined with new seeds of opportunity, led to a beautiful harvest.

CHAPTER 6

DESPERATION

It's a late night in the '90s. David Goggins is just getting off his shift of spraying down restaurants with pesticide. His routine is to pick up a pack of donuts and an extra-large chocolate shake and plop himself down on his couch in front of his TV.

He had fallen out of his dream and was at a point of desperation.

He had a vision for himself to become part of the Air Force Pararescue. Goggins excelled at just about every physical discipline, except water confidence. His uncalloused mind filled him with doubt as he struggled in the water. When he saw a way out through medical leave due to having the sickle cell anemia trait, he took it and started to go into a dark place. A place where he was a zombie, just going through the motions of life, not working toward his dream of being in a special unit of the military.

After Air Force bootcamp in 1994, he was lean at 175 lbs. By 1999, he was a husky 290.[26] His old crappy apartment was analogous to his mind's prison: a place of desperation where he could feel comfortably numb.

He got off the couch and headed to the shower; he could hear the TV from across the hall. "Navy seals... toughest... the world..." He rushed from the bathroom to the TV to see a show that demonstrated the lives of Basic Underwater Demolition SEAL (BUD/S) Training Class 224. They were going through Hell Week, the most arduous series of tasks in the most physically demanding training in the military.

"In a society where mediocrity is too often the standard and too often rewarded," said their commanding officer, "there is intense fascination with the men who detest mediocrity, who refuse to define themselves in conventional terms, and who seek to transcend traditionally recognized human capabilities. This is exactly the type of person BUD/S is meant to find. The man who finds a way to complete each task to the best of his ability. The man who will adapt and overcome any and all obstacles."

This little bit of inspiration was what Goggins needed to get out of what he described as a "mental hell" to move along a path of resistance to realize his conviction of becoming a Navy SEAL. It was at this moment Goggins had a reawakening to join a special forces unit.

---

26   David Goggins, *Can't Hurt Me* (Austin: Lioncrest Publishing, 2018), 85.

At the same time, it was this place of desperation that sealed the deal to quit his job at Ecolab. After a particularly horrible night of rats, roaches, and raccoons, he dropped his gear, went home and put on a pair of sweats, and started running.

When we get to a point so low, we feel we need to change to survive. Ideally, we should find a piece of inspiration to set us down our paths to fulfill our personal legend, but it is important to recognize our lowest point to leverage us to change.

For Goggins, his piece of inspiration was watching Navy SEALS go through Hell Week. Seeing how they took the worst the world had thrown at them and kept coming back for more ignited him to re-enlist and achieve a greater purpose of joining a special forces military unit.

He cut his weight and passed the tests to qualify for the Navy SEALS, went through "Hell Week" three times, and on the third attempt made it in. He is the only person to ever go through three hell weeks.

A question we must ask ourselves to make a change is, where can our inspiration come from? What can it look like? What can set us on a path to propel ourselves to be our very best selves, whatever that looks like?

At the end of the day, inspiration can hit us at any time, whether we are watching TV or having pests pour over us. It is how we grab onto it and let it take us somewhere we want to go.

Goggins knew he wanted to be a SEAL: he had his feeling of that greater purpose. He had his defining moment of inspiration from watching BUD/S go through a course that pushed you to the max and then some. Finally, his vision of becoming a SEAL allowed him to create an intense fitness and study plan that guided him to getting accepted into the program and fueling him to continue when his mind wanted to give out on him.

When we reach a point in desperation, our eyes can adjust to the darkness and we begin to live day to day, abandoning our vision, if we ever even had one. When we are in our low point, however, it's never too late to get back up.

Sometimes it takes just a little bit of inspiration to get the stone rolling. Eventually that stone will gain momentum and pick up speed, until ultimately we are quickly racing back towards our vision. If the mountain we are rolling down is high enough, we may have enough momentum to carry us over the next hill.

***

Before COVID-19 hit, I volunteered as an adult tutor at the downtown branch of the Seattle Public Library. I worked with an elderly couple from Cartagena, Colombia, who had moved to Seattle to be closer to their son who worked at Microsoft. They described Cartagena as a beautiful walled city, each building and house its own color, looking into the Caribbean Sea.

I had it on my list of places I wanted to visit for a while, and it was very much a "why the hell not" moment. I departed from SeaTac on March fourth and spent the first week in Cartagena.

Arriving in Cartagena, I realized that COVID-19 was a global concern. Half the travelers in the airport were wearing masks and all on staff had their face covered.

The first thing I saw after I got off the airplane into the terminal was a booth advertising Corona beer. I don't think anyone wanted a Corona at this time. Before getting into the terminal, the airport faculty checked everyone's temperature to make sure none of us were running a fever.

I was not sure if it actually worked or if there was a quarantine protocol in place at this early point, but the nerves were building as it became my turn to get my temperature checked. The fellow passengers were moving quickly as their ears received a "beep" and were signaled to move along.

My turn. She pointed the thermometer gun at my ear. Pulled the trigger. "Beep."

I took my first step into Colombia.

I was intending on spending my entire eleven-day trip to Colombia in Cartagena, but the travelers I ran into highly encouraged me to visit some of the other cities, and if I had enough time I should go to Medellin.

On March 10, 2020, I arrived in Medellin, Colombia. The coronavirus was heating up around the globe, with hundreds of new cases popping up around the world every day. When I left for Colombia, everyone was unsure how to react to this unseen demon covering the world, how serious it was, and if it was the apocalypse to start raiding for.

On March 11, it was officially listed as a pandemic, and it was a global conversation. *Maybe I'll have to cut my vacation short.* There weren't too many cases in Colombia, significantly fewer than in Seattle, the city I was living in at the time. *I only have a few more days here, might as well stick it out.*

This was right before quarantine started. I didn't realize that this time in Medellin would be my last moments of normalcy before the whole world went on lockdown. At one point I was considering extending my vacation and spending additional time in Colombia. My company made the announcement to work remotely on March 9, which seemed like a dream. Almost like a snow day. I'm really glad I wasn't too bold and took my flight back to the US on the 16th. The same day I had scheduled to leave the country, they officially went into quarantine.

Days before, on the roof of Los Patios Hotel, a weekly party was going on. I was greeted by a young, short, toasted Colombian who offered me an Aguila beer. I took the frosty beverage and made my way through the crowd toward the edge of the roof to catch a glimpse of the Medellin skyline. I squeezed through two Dutchmen and finally caught some fresh air by sticking my head over the edge of the building. I was standing next to a young man smoking a cigarette with bushy hair.

By the look of his flip-flops, cargo shorts, and Hawaiian shirt, I could tell he was on vacation as well.

He offered me a cigarette as we got to know each other. His name was Peter and he was a drummer in a band in the Czech Republic.

Among the stress he had from getting extorted by cops in Mexico, now he was worried about how he was going to get home. "Trump has blocked access to the US from any European citizen, I have a connecting flight through New York; I do not know if I am able to take that flight."

There was a lot of confusion in the air that night. As I shuffled from one group to the next, met traveler after traveler, everyone was unsure what the future was going to look like. Many were worried for their loved ones. Many were worried about how the pandemic and quarantining would affect the overall global economy. I happened to run into two travelers from Houston who were grieving over the Houston Rodeo being canceled.

The world was ending, but dammit, I was on vacation: I was going to find something to do if it killed me.

COMUNA 13

When I asked around, everyone suggested to go on a free walking tour of Comuna 13. I didn't know much about it prior to going in, other than it used to be a dangerous spot but now has some very cool graffiti.

I took the light rail from El Poblando to San Javier, the neighborhood that cradles Comuna 13. I stepped out of the station and was approached by several tour guides, most of them speaking Spanish. As a traveler, you always need to be on the lookout from getting scammed or pickpocketed, so I cautiously approached the guides and said "Inglés?". Eventually, someone noticed my confused gringo demeanor and tried talking to me in English: "Hola! Are you here for tour?"

I said yes and flashed my walking tour confirmation ticket, and they directed me to a young Afro-Colombian man. I walked up to him, showed him my ticket. He introduced himself as Christian and told me to wait next to a grocery store with the rest of the tourists as more attendees funneled in.

About ten minutes passed, and he gave us the rundown of what to expect before herding us onto a bus. He emphasized not to get separated from the group, as the labyrinth of Comuna 13 made it easy to get lost, and though being a safe tourist attraction during the day, it was not a place you wanted to be in at night.

We got off the bus and began the tour.

Just outside of Medellin, Comuna 13 is a small neighborhood resembling one of Brazil's favelas. This neighborhood is known for its winding and uphill streets. An easy place to get lost and avoid police, it became notorious for groups loyal to drug lords such as Pablo Escobar in the '80s and '90s.

Christian described growing up during this time: many of the residents lived in poverty and terror, not knowing how they were going to make money to buy food or when the next shooting was going to happen. Members of the groups noticed this and leveraged it to recruit the young people for their efforts.

"I will give you new shoes, new clothes, and one million pesos, all of that and you will get the reputation that comes from working in our crew." This is what the members would tell them, and a lot of young people, with no better way to make money, would join them out of desperation.

"Man, get out of here black boy!" the gang members told Christian when he declined their offer. All of Christian's friends that joined were killed by police or other gangs.

He took us up several escalators, describing the graffiti along the way. It told the story of the people of Comuna 13, its dark times, those who stepped up as community leaders, and the 2002 police raid Operation Orion which involved over one thousand policemen, soldiers, and helicopters to overthrow the groups that had made the neighborhood one of the most dangerous in the world.

There was so much art it's hard to say in words what was on display. One piece showed the layers of flesh of a dark-skinned woman: the top layer of skin, the muscles beneath, and the skeletal system. Discrimination has been a problem in Colombia; the artist was exhibiting that under the skin we are all made of the same stuff.

Comuna 13 acts as a canvas for artists across Colombia. Sidling past the other tourists and hugging the wall, letting locals on scooters zoom by, the graffiti I was pressed up against was looking down at me.

A half-gold, half-turquoise lion. It made me think of power. Christian said the lion was drawn by many artists, and if you look closely, the lion is comprised of many different animals.

The higher we scaled into the neighborhood, a colorful rendition of Michael Jackson hid his eyes from us, while Scrooge McDuck casually smoked a cigar as some dollar bills floated around him.

When we reached the apex of the neighborhood, a cute avocado waved at us with the words "No hay un problema que no se solucione con un aguacate."

"There isn't a problem that can't be fixed with an avocado."
-@iamthetrece

From here you could see the rolling hills of the Comuna 13 favela. With all the buildings blending into a brick ocean, you could see the Medellin skyline in the horizon.

Graffiti isn't the only art in Comuna 13. A young tan Colombian shared an elaborate handshake with Christian as my group sat down on a row of laid-out foldable chairs.

Christian translated: he wanted words from us. Words that meant something. People shouted out their land. "Amsterdam! London! Aruba! Venezuela!"

"HOUSTON!" I screeched.

The young man wrote all these words on a whiteboard and a beat started playing. He started freestyling in Spanish, incorporating all the places we loved into his flow.

He must have performed for ten minutes before taking a bow. After the show, Christian translated so I could have a conversation with him.

The young man came from nothing, was involved with the characters that made Comuna 13 a dangerous place and did some things he regrets.

Overall, though, he is happy to be alive and uses his story to create music to be someone.

***

Those who grew up in Comuna 13 at the time illustrate how desperation pushes people to make a change.

In our lives, we may at times find ourselves in states of desperation.

When we are in this state, it tends to bring about a deep sense of self reflection. We analyze how we got here, who's to blame, and how we could have done things differently, and we wish things could be different. Often, we argue that things are unfair.

However, when we are in an unfavorable situation, whether it be our own doing or circumstance, we are the ones who need to act in order to pull ourselves out.

"If it is meant to be, it is up to me." There's some debate on the origination of that quote, but the meaning is priceless. If we are to get to a better place in life, we must hold ourselves accountable. We cannot wait for things to get better. Just because we were dealt a bad hand does not mean we can't look through the deck and get a favorable hand; we have to work with what we got.

Those in Comuna 13 who survived the bad times are doing better. After the dust settled and several raids from the military police, it has become a popular tourist destination in Medellin, attracting thousands of visitors a week from all over the world.

Christian said no to the gangsters and took a few beatings, as declining their invitation was disrespectful. Now, Christian can make millions of pesos a week working for tips as a tour guide.

Desperation is a low point often coupled with negative thoughts that keep us there. One thing that can help guide us out of darkness is a little light. That little light can come in many different forms. Sometimes a little faith can act as a candle that can lead us through the darkness.

CHAPTER 7

HAVE FAITH

———

NOT WHAT I EXPECTED

Growing up, I did not want to be an entrepreneur. I did not want to be a salesman or, god forbid, a writer. What really made my eyes wide was what I thought a geologist did.

Starting at around five or six, I was obsessed with rocks, minerals, and any form of matter that I could add to my rock collection. Day after day I would study the classification of rocks. Metamorphic, igneous, sedimentary, quartz, any different type of rock I could find, I would add to my collection, especially the shiny ones.

I don't know what it was that fascinated me with rocks—perhaps that there are so many to be cataloged? Maybe it was the pretty colors? Maybe it was because some were shiny? Regardless, I loved to collect and learn about these chunks of earth.

When I was around fourteen, I shared with one of my teachers my interest in becoming a geologist, as they are the ones who study rocks.

"That's a good profession, they make a lot of money in the oil and gas industry," said my eighth-grade science teacher.

Oil and gas... I don't give a hoot about oil and gas, I thought. *I just want to look at rocks all day.*

Growing up in Houston, a major oil city, every bit of evidence I found seemed to have a geologist work in this sector. "Geologists look at the structural and sedimentary aspects of the stratum/strata to identify possible oil traps." I glazed over this in Wikipedia. *Maybe this isn't really what I want.*

So there I was, fourteen and lost again.

Fifteen came around. High school sucked. For the usual reasons, teen angst and being new to a school of more than three thousand kids was no fun at all.

If there was one defining moment in high school, it was my legendary *The Hound of the Baskervilles* improvised classroom presentation. One of Sir Arthur Conan Doyle's entries in his *Sherlock Holmes* series, my assignment was to present an alternate ending to the story. I didn't have an actual one written down, so when called upon to present I could have either taken the late grade or had fun with presenting.

I remember facing the whiteboard, taking a deep breath, and going off with a satire I had written in my head just a few hours before. I can't recall exactly what I ad-libbed, and it probably wouldn't be as funny anyway, but I do remember the reaction of the classroom.

The roaring laughter, the energy from getting the first couple of giggles—I was truly crushing it with this audience. The class applauded upon conclusion and my teacher let me turn in the assignment a day late without any penalties. The draft is probably lost on a flash drive somewhere, like a forgotten bunch of bitcoins decaying in a dump, and although the words are lost now, the experience was timeless.

That day, I figured out something I truly enjoyed doing— presenting.

So, at the time I figured I could have fun when presenting. I would say from that point on about fifty percent of my presentations have gone well: quieting the audience with a loud voice, keeping the audience involved by asking questions, and keeping them awake by sprinkling in humor. Forty percent are mediocre but good, touching all the points of a successful presentation but not getting that electrifying feeling of what stand-up comedians call *killing.* The other ten percent is what comedians refer to as *bombing.*

At one point I even considered becoming a stand-up comedian, and even to this day, I want to pursue humor. I may not have enough material to get on stage just yet, but what I do know is that whatever I continue to do in the future, I want to ride the wave of an energetic crowd.

***

HAKEEM THE DREAM

When I got my first job working at my family's car stereo shop, I was excited to finally start working yet disinterested in the industry. But to get good at any job, you need to learn.

Day after day, I would talk to customers and sell them easy things like tires and window tint. I would watch the more experienced sales reps talk to customers about custom installations, complicated wiring setups for various configurations of speaker systems and amplifiers, and watch them turn replacing new speakers into a fully integrated sound system with speakers, subwoofers, amp, and Double Din head unit with installation to rack up some pretty pricey deals.

I spent a majority of my summer days during school working there. The days would seem to drag on forever, especially during the month of Ramadan. My uncle Hasan was a manager; I call him Uncle Sam.

Uncle Sam fasted every day during the month of Ramadan. I fasted once and it was tough. It wasn't the hunger that bothered me; it was the thirst. Being dehydrated and dealing with feisty customers was a difficult task.

Sometimes customers made things difficult when things didn't go according to plan and they had some additional wait time. Periodically, they would even blow up. But the worst was when customers didn't come in. When business is slow, it really feels like time is standing still. And when there's no business, you're not making money. And when a sales rep isn't making money then the company isn't making money, which leads to rumors of layoffs.

Bored and on edge, the humid summer days in Houston felt like they would last forever. If there is one piece of advice I could give to my younger self, it would to be: learn to love this moment. Sure, it might kind of suck in some ways now, but you're surrounded by people who love and support you, and you have the freedom to go out and do whatever you want. The future is uncertain, but you can form your vision and take control of your destiny.

I even tell myself that now, sure you can't go out and do whatever the hell you want right now, but when you're back in the office slouching in your chair and have more responsibilities, you're gonna miss the work-from-home saga.

When I was a lad working in Car Stereo, that excitement was more anxiety, and waiting for those customers, the humidity and thirst and hunger putting me to sleep, the moment was slowly lulling me into a grave.

Uncle Sam noticed this, and being the old amiable Arab he is, he started to talk about his earlier days in car stereo and his first years in Houston in the 1990s.

"Did you know I used to go to the mosque with Hakeem Olajuwon?" said Uncle Sam, leaning back in his chair as we both waited for a customer to walk in.

"Oh really…" I skeptically answered.

"Oh yeah! After his games he would come to the mosque and pray. I stood right next to him once," Uncle Sam said enthusiastically.

"Did you say hi to him or get a picture with him?" I said, straightening my back while spinning on the barstool I was sitting on.

"C'mon man, this was the '90s, we didn't have picture phones on us all the time. I said hi and we spoke for a bit. In Arabic! Did you know he was playing games while fasting? He led the Rockets to victory in the '95 championships while fasting!"

It is hard to believe someone was able to square off against some of the best, like Michael Jordan and Charles Barkley, running on fumes. But it's true: Hakeem played many games for the Houston Rockets with nothing but a date and a glass of water in the morning in his system. In those two years where the rockets won the '94 and '95 championships, Hakeem scored a higher amount of points on average during the month of Ramadan versus the games of the season that were not during Ramadan.

So, the question is, how do Hakeem and others derive power from faith? Does God or some power give him the edge he needs to take a game away from Michael Jordan? Maybe. Or maybe he believes that such a power is being granted to him, enough that it creates a placebo effect for him to make fewer mistakes against the greatest basketball players of the '90s.

Is this really that hard of an idea to believe? We see placebo belief giving strength to individuals everywhere.

"The placebo effect is more than positive thinking—believing a treatment or procedure will work. It's about creating a stronger connection between the brain and body and how they work together," says Professor Ted Kaptchuk of Harvard-affiliated Beth Israel Deaconess Medical Center, whose research focuses on the placebo effect.[27]

In the culture-shifting basketball film *Space Jam*, Michael Jordan plays himself making a return to basketball by saving Looney Toon Land from the Monstars. The Looney Toons don't believe they can defeat the MonStars, who have stolen the talent from Muggsy Bogues, Larry Johnson, Charles Barkley, Patrick Ewing, and Shawn Bradley until Michael gives them a taste of "Mike's Secret Stuff" (which is just a bottle of water). He tells them this formula gives him the ability to be a hard-in-the-paint basketball player. They believe and are given the confidence in themselves for them to defeat the Monstars and save Looney Toon Land.[28]

In addition to children's films, we see this in the real world as well.

MMA fighter Sage Northcutt is an example. Sage is one of the youngest fighters to ever compete in the UFC, and one of his driving motivators is his belief in Christianity.

---

27 "The power of the placebo effect." *Harvard Health Publishing*, last modified August 9, 2019.

28 *Space Jam*, directed by Joe Pytka, featuring Michael Jordan (Burbank, CA: Warner Bros, 1996).

"I'm blessed by God to be here," says Sage in many of his post-fight interviews.[29]

Was it God that gave him the strength to swarm and beat the crap out of his opponent? Again, maybe. Across sports, many say religious faith grants a leg up on the competition.

"I think religious faith gives athletes an edge in the sense that they believe that everything happens for a reason and they are going to be protected," Penn State women's gymnastics coach Steve Shephard said.

Another way of putting it is the belief in their faith is so great that it spills out into their own abilities. With such intense faith, Sage can quickly end fights, and Hakeem is able to play at his best despite being hungry and thirsty from fasting.

It makes sense: if God sees it in your future that you will win, and you truly believe that, you can definitely walk into the octagon or onto the court with confidence. We see faith playing a role many times in history. Malcolm X discovered Islam while in prison, and his eagerness to learn and walk the way of Mohamed put him on a path of reading books for fifteen hours a day.

"Reporters would ask me if I got my degree from Harvard or one of those other schools, but my education was completely self-taught from reading books from the prison library."

---

29 *UFC - Ultimate Fighting Championship,* "UFC 192: Sage Northcutt Octagon Interview & Highlights," October 3, 2015, video, 2:04.

His strong belief in Islam had him do many things in his rise to prominence.

Religion is probably the best-known medium to cultivate faith and belief, but it is not the only way belief can be developed.

Nick Yaris, for example, believed in an idea. Nick lived a hellish life being on death row for twenty-two years and contemplated killing himself many times. Nick was a victim of the prison-industrial complex.

"I've been shot, stabbed, strangled, run over by a car, hung myself in prison, two drug overdoses, and I had a cannibal try to murder me for two solid years. I know that I could fall at any moment from my own hand. But God bless me, I believe so much in my purpose in life that I will not kill myself. I won't give up. And it's only because I've been tested that I know that has to be for a reason."[30]

Nick wanted to get his story out there. He wanted to expose the corrupt prison-industrial complex: how an innocent man could be put in jail by false testimony and little evidence. His goal was to make sure no innocent man was ever put in a situation like him ever again. His belief in his mission kept him alive through his darkest years. He's now a successful book author, documenting the story of twenty-two years on death row.

---

30 *A2Z Production,* "Joe Rogan - CRAZY Death Row Story by Nick Yarris," September 12, 2018. video, 39:00.

If you truly believe in yourself, the path forward will be more clear to you, you can be confident in the work you are doing, confident that you will succeed, and see a setback as part of "God's plan" and move forward.

Believing in yourself can be hard, so learning how to believe is a school of thought all on its own with some undeniably real benefits.

In short, faith creates belief, and this belief can be channeled into ourselves to pursue our visions. We learn from athletes and visionaries the extent to which their belief-derived faith empowered them to live out their visions and be someone.

CHAPTER 8

TRAGEDY AND CHANGE

"I've been acting like this because I can't take these shutdowns anymore and I'm scared of what it's doing to me. I'm looking for who to blame, saying I'm trying to help people to make myself feel better, but the truth is, I just want to have fun again. I wanted to see if it was possible to go out in the world and do things the way that I used to, but it isn't. I'm not any better and I don't care any more than anyone else. I did this because I just want my life back."

-STAN MARSH, *SOUTH PARK*

Who better to share what kids in 2020 are feeling than Stan Marsh of *South Park*.

Surprisingly, most content produced in the COVID-19 era does not acknowledge the virus' existence. If you think about it, every story written today that does not acknowledge COVID-19 and that it affects day to day life runs on an alternate timeline. It feels like a lot of content produced nowadays idealizes the past.

Kids all over the world are stuck in a strange position where adults do not know how to take care of them. The pandemic disrupted school, which for the most part has been facilitated online. Students aren't getting the same experience and are missing out on making new friends and participating in extracurriculars, and even going outside has increased barriers to entry.

My little brother, still in school, describes it as "school but just with the boring parts."

Indeed, this pandemic has been a tragedy for all of us, but students may have had it the worst. Exploring the world and learning for yourself what's out there has slowed down. Learning from the education system is only a byproduct.

"The only source of knowledge is experience."

-ALBERT EINSTEIN

The less we experience, the less we learn. Your 20s and below are your learning years, and time is one thing that you can't get back.

RESILIENCE

Most of us experience tragedies at some point in our lives. They shake us to our very core and can change the way we see the world. They are moments of suffering, typically associated with some form of loss.

Tragedies affect us in different ways. We grieve. We get depressed. We isolate ourselves. We shut others out. We feel angry. We want to alter what we are feeling. We want to escape. We change to survive our thoughts.

Whether it directly affects ourselves or loved ones, a tragedy can be a very powerful source of change.

In fact, if one were to assume that the more considerable the impact an event has on us can lead to the greatest change, then tragedy is the greatest source of change. This can ultimately lead to self-destruction, too, which is why it is the greatest test for humans—to rise from a fall.

Resilience has been most frequently defined as positive adaptation despite adversity.[31] In many cases, those who handle tragedy are some the most resilient people.

Dr. Jana Pressley, director of training and professional development at the Trauma Center and an adjunct associate professor at Richmont Graduate University, believes those who survive complex trauma are some of the most resilient.

"Take one of my patients who was severely neglected and never learned to self soothe; he had to be chronically high or hospitalized to stay alive for his first thirty years of life. As a first step, this young man learned to regulate himself in crisis and stayed out of the hospital for a year…and that was what resilience looked like for him."[32]

---

31   John Fleming and Robert J. Ledogar, "Resilience, an Evolving Concept: A Review of Literature Relevant to Aboriginal Research," *Canada Institutes of Health Research*, (Summer 2008): 6(2): 7–23.

32   Jamie D. Aten, "What Resilience Looks Like in Complex Trauma," *Psychology Today*, April 10, 2019.

Tragic events are nearly always out of our control, so leveraging them to make changes is quite difficult. The aftermath is an extremely stressful, demoralizing, anxiety-filled time: a period that's difficult to navigate, let alone to leverage in a positive way. However, if you can survive the experience, coming out on the other side as a stronger person with a renewed look on life is possible.

GRAND OPENING

The music blared in the celebration for the grand opening of the Abdoun Circle location of Arafat Sweets. Right next to the McDonald's, it was prime real estate in one of the most well-developed parts of Amman, Jordan. My dad would always call me Mr. Adam and I would call him Mr. Bill. Mr. Bill was pulled away from us by some suited Arabs to discuss business.

This was the third grand opening I had been to this month, but it was possibly the most anticipated one. The mayor of Amman was there, as were some famous Arab singers, and there was a camera crew capturing the whole thing.

I wasn't too into the sweets at the time; an eleven-year-old from the States tends to be picky on what they eat. At the time I would prefer chocolate cake and cookies over kunafa and baklava. The syrupy cheese and flaky, sticky phyllo dough layered with pistachios sweets were so different than the fluffy, flour-based, chocolaty sweets I had come to love in the US.

"Why you no want to speak on TV?" the reporter said to me in a thick Arabic accent as he was walking out with his crew. I wasn't really interested in staying at the event. I would much rather have been in my room playing on my bootlegged PS2. If there was one good thing I was experiencing at the time of living in Jordan, it was the bootlegged video games for 1.50 JD.

HOMESICK

On my first day at the Abdul Hamid Sharaf School—also known as AHSS, better known as ASS—I picked out a desk in the far back corner of my homeroom class. "Yo, yo, yo, check out the cool kid in the back," quacked my dad. I don't even know how he found my classroom. I was already on the other side of the world away from the state of Texas I called home, so things in my eyes couldn't get much worse.

I was the Arafat kid. The kid whose family owned all the Arafat Sweets. One day my dad had one of our workers bring in Kunafa fingers for show and tell. Most of my classmates were super excited when they arrived; I was happy they liked them, but I did not want a piece myself.

In the AHSS school system you get break, not lunch and recess like in the American school system. I sat down under a tree and began to munch on some leftover pizza from last night. I remember feeling so sad. So alone. So different. The only kid not from here. I didn't speak Arabic, nor was I extroverted. It was a tough transition.

I had asked Mr. Bill and my mom many times why we moved to Jordan. He said for a better life. Mom said he got in a fight with his brother over ownership of our car stereo stores in Houston and wanted to prove that he didn't need him to run a business.

Whatever it was, it happened. A lot of things lined up right—whether part of an intended strategy or just sheer luck, I am still unsure of.

In May 2005, the name Arafat was very recognizable; this was due in part to the death of the Palestinian Liberation Organization Chairman, Yasser Arafat, in fall of 2004. Mr. Bill said the name was the Middle Eastern equivalent to Starbucks. Maybe that was what inspired him to grow the business at such a quick speed.

I am not sure what the prime motivating factor pushing him to jump on this dream was, whether it was ego, opportunity, or inspiration. Personally, I think it was all three.

I do know that this entrepreneurial endeavor left an impact on me and my family.

It was an experience that allowed us to live in an entirely different culture; an experience that, when we moved back to the US, made us appreciate all the luxuries we have here: pretty green grass lawns, being able to drink water from the tap, not having to go through metal detectors at the mall. An experience that stirred what was the genesis of my entrepreneurial spirit. I'm not sure if my Dad planned on this, but going to all those grand openings really inspired me.

Looking back at the early days growing up in Jordan, for the longest time I felt frustrated. I felt my time spent here robbed me of my coming-of-age years. I felt that it stunted my social growth, making the remainder of my secondary school career unenjoyable.

What I learned from this is that you shouldn't wait for things to get better. I waited three years to move back to the United States, but when I came back, it never really felt like home. To this day I still have dreams of returning home, wherever that is.

I learned you must steer into the skid.

Skids happen; if you embrace them, life will be an adventure instead of a tragedy.[33]

✳✳✳

THE LIGHT AT THE END OF THE TUNNEL

There's no easy way of dealing with a tragedy. There's no telling if one will truly get over a death of a loved one or losing a job. What we do know is that life goes on. With that we need to ask ourselves the hard question: is there anything to take away from this? Is it possible to use this experience as a vehicle for meaningful change?

---

33 Michael Karson, "Turn in the Direction of the Skid," *Psychology Today*, November 9, 2013.

"You can't go back and change the beginning, but you can start where you are and change the ending."

-C.S. Lewis

The ability to come back from tragedies with minimal negative outcome is called resilience. Some people develop resilience growing up and going through adversity.

The weight gained from a tragic experience can arguably never be shed. Like a heavy backpack we carry around, we cannot hope for the bag to get lighter, but we can hope to get stronger. Like scaling a mountain, we cannot count on the terrain to get easier, we must count on ourselves to get stronger.

PART 3

WHAT LIES AHEAD

Life is not about waiting for the storm to pass,
it's about learning to dance in the rain.
VIVIAN GREENE

CHAPTER 9

THE NEW NORMAL

DISORGANIZED

June 27, 2020. It's been three months since the COVID-19 pandemic hit the world.

Hair? Cut it once every three months. Belly? Round from not going to the gym and a fast food diet. Meat? Beat like it can't pay its gambling debts.

I'm still working from home at my West Coast tech job. Many of my colleagues in Houston who worked in oil and gas are looking for a new job.

My schedule has changed so much since March 2020. My routine has gone out the window, for better and for worse. I don't have to wake up at 6:30 a.m. anymore to catch the bus downtown. My commute has shrunk from forty-five minutes to less than five seconds. Walking to the bus stop, waiting for the bus, and dealing with traffic on the way downtown has been replaced with rolling out of bed and taking three steps to my desk.

My routine fell into place. Reading, exercising, and writing, among other hobbies. Like a well-run machine, I would follow the protocol, and I felt satisfied with it.

But then the world changed, and not in the way the speaker at your high school graduation said it would. Unexpectedly, it isolated us from our peers, like a snow day that has gone on for the better part of a year.

Trying to build a new routine in 2020, what a lot of people are dubbing as "the new normal" continues to be a big challenge for me. What held me accountable was my schedule, which revolved around work and destinations.

I would go to the office, go to a Brazilian Jiu-Jitsu gym, go to salsa lessons at a dance studio, and would read on the bus and at coffee shops.

Now, the biggest adventure I take during the weekday is my trip to the grocery store. Keeping my distance, following the six-feet-apart stickers placed on the floor. No accountability to be social. Being social is seen as disrespect in 2020 to those who are vulnerable to the virus.

If you aren't wearing a mask, social distancing, and minimizing your exposure to the general public, you are seen as an a**hole.

What a time to be alive.

WASTING TIME

I have seen a sharp increase in time spent on my phone. One day I logged in over six hours! Looks like I found out where most of my freed-up time went.

The deconstruction of my routine has left me in a state of disorganization. I want to read, but the motivation isn't there. I want to write stories for this book, but inspiration isn't there. I want to work out, but the discipline isn't there.

They say you shouldn't rely on motivation, that discipline is the key to getting stuff done. Motivation comes and goes, but discipline is something developed that doesn't go away.

For me it was routine.

I used to go to a boxing and BJJ class four times a week. That routine has gone out the window. I haven't replaced it with anything.

I had a ten-year goal of becoming a black belt; that seems unlikely now. My vision that I have to be someone has had a serious wrench thrown in it.

Adjusting to this new normal has been difficult.

The Roman emperor Marcus Aurelius said, "What stands in the way becomes the way." If we are to find our vision in the new normal, we cannot just wait for a fairytale ending of Corona to happen.

Because let's be honest—even if there is a vaccine that negates the virus, distribution will take time, people will be scared to travel—things have changed, and they will stay that way for a while.

With stay-at-home orders morphing into de facto law, the need to be someone has few outlets.

To form a vision to satisfy the need to be someone, we need to be excited about the work toward it. We need to rewire our reward system to pull us to our vision.

I get passionate and excited about many things, but nothing quite got my heart racing like this one dream I had.

FANTASY

I had gotten away with something heinous, I think a robbery: perhaps I looted a bank or a train. Regardless, I remember being chased, thinking I was safe at one moment, then having to scramble from my hiding spot because whatever authority or criminal I ripped off kept catching up with me.

I remember feeling terror the entire time, until I reached safety, stumbling into a small apartment through a window and hearing the steps of whoever was chasing me fade away into the distance. I remember vividly this fear turning into excitement.

Then I woke up.

Occasionally this dream will drift into my head again. I don't remember the exact details but rather the feeling I experienced.

I felt powerful, like I had proved something. It's hard to describe the feeling of getting away with making millions from one bank heist or to know even if that feeling I felt was real.

It felt good. I can't remember a time in my life I felt something like that before. I wonder to myself, what can I do to recreate that feeling?

Should I attempt to rob a bank or a jewelry store? Probably not, I do not think that would end up well for me. But what could I do to recreate the rush of robbing something and getting away with it? Does life even offer people the chance to experience something like this?

Can this feeling of exhilaration only be achieved by doing something so drastically life altering that if you fail it could negatively impact your life forever? If you get caught robbing a bank, you go to jail, and probably for a long time. If you try to rip off a mob dealer, you sleep with the fishes.

Are risking high stakes the only way to achieve this feeling? Is there any way to achieve this rush without doing something illegal or a risk of dying? I hope so: never have I felt so alive but in dead sleep.

Maybe we can learn something from Eddie Chapman, a British double agent who fed misinformation to Nazi Germany.

ZIGZAG

"Chapman loved himself, loved adventure, and loved his country, probably in that order."

-MI5 OFFICER'S ASSESSMENT

Eddie Chapman was your run-of-the-mill English gangster before the second world war broke out. He was a member of the "jelly gang," a group of criminals that specialized in using gelignite gel to blast open safes.

He eventually got caught, served some time, and upon release made his way to the Jersey Channel Islands. It was here he got involved in more petty crime and was eventually tracked down having dinner with his lover at Hotel de la Page when he was approached by Jersey Island authorities. He alluded them by jumping out the window—which was closed—and committed one more burglary. After that, once caught, they sentenced him to jail for two years.

During his sentence, the Germans invaded the Channel Islands. Chapman was transferred to Paris and convinced German command that he would act as an agent for them and sabotage the English. They agreed and trained him in explosives, communications, and parachuting. They sent him off to England, parachuting him in, and once he landed, he immediately surrendered himself to British police and was turned over to MI5, the English intelligence agency.

Chapman convinced the English to let him act as an agent for them to triple-cross the Germans. MI5 agreed and set him off on a journey to destroy false facilities and feed the Germans misinformation. He became known as ZigZag for his checkered past and tendency to zigzag back and forth on the line of morality.

He fed fake intelligence to the Germans by staging a sabotage of a British airplane factory, allowing the allies to have more air support.

Even after the war, he felt the need to commit crimes such as smuggling gold across the Mediterranean and kidnapping the Sultan of Morocco.[34]

What drove Chapman? Why was he so adamant about getting into trouble? Why did he persist and keep getting himself into these situations?

The way Chapman lived his life is quite the opposite of the average person.

Holding yourself accountable to an everyday routine, most of it spent at home, is not very exciting.

"The thing about repairing, maintaining, and cleaning is: it's not an adventure. There's no way to do it so wrong you might die. It's just work. And the bottom line is some people are

---

34 "A spy who loved himself: the story of Eddie Chapman – a double agent, a smuggler, a swindler and a womanizer," *Hybrid Tech Car* (blog), accessed October 12, 2020.

okay going to work, and some people...Well, some people would rather die," to quote Dan Harmon's *Rick and Morty*.[35]

BRINGING BACK SCHOOL PERIODS

If I were to define what my perfect routine would look like in 2020, being stuck at home, I think my schedule would look like my high school schedule. Biology, theater, algebra, lunch, English, history, and track. However, instead of taking classes, I would fill my schedule with something I have been planning on doing for years but just haven't gotten around to doing because I am too "busy."

Now that I am not busy, isn't it time to not let any of the excuses get in my way and "go back to school?"

Squeezing it into my work schedule, this is what I would expect my schedule to look like:

6:30 a.m. Wake Up
7:00 a.m. Exercise
8:00 a.m. Shower/Coffee
8:15 a.m. Work
12:00 a.m. Read/Lunch
1:00 a.m. More Work
4:00 a.m. Language Course
5:00 a.m. Guitar Lesson
6:00 a.m. Write
7:30 a.m. Chill Time/Dinner/Room for Activities

---

35   *Rick and Morty*, season 3, episode 3, "Pickle Rick," created by Dan Harmon, aired August 6, 2017, on Adult Swim.

Work would be a class on its own, a triple period with it taking most of my day. Reading, the language course, and the guitar course would be three extra "classes" to fill my schedule. The challenge comes from doing any of this. It's easier said than done.

In reality, my day to day looks like:

8:00 a.m. Wake Up
8:31 a.m. Get out of bed and hop onto my first Zoom meeting of the day, late.
9:00 a.m. Work; scattered emails, a phone call or two, browsing all of my social media despite just closing it, random YouTube videos in the background; they used to be funny but have gotten so far down the rabbit hole that they are just weird and surreal.
12:00 p.m. Take a shower for some reason.
12:30 p.m. Make sandwich, eat, eat, and eat some more.
2:00 p.m. Do something with work to make yourself feel like you have done something productive.
4:00 p.m. Feel anxious that I have not done enough.
4:01 p.m. Chill time?

Sadly, the second schedule seems to win often. Why is that? Why do I break away from the schedule and not stick to the routine I envisioned for myself?

This goes to the conundrum of long versus short-term thinking. For example, eating unhealthily is an easier option than meal planning, grocery shopping, and nutrient portioning.

Long term has better payoffs, but you must do uncomfortable work that could be considered challenging, boring, and unrewarding. The worst feeling is when you are working on something but you feel like you are doing it wrong and are not making any progress.

For example, writing a book. Looking at a chapter as a blank canvas, trying to approach it as an artist and creating something beautiful, it just ends up in chaos.

With no guiding structure on how to build a compelling chapter or experience to fall back on (present company included), you inevitably fail at making any progress. You just wonder, how did I manage to waste another day of accomplishing nothing?

Not a single drop of dopamine is earned. So, you get pushed into this place of stagnation, doing little things that give you a little hit of that good-good.

"Dopamine plays a role in how we feel pleasure. It's a big part of our unique human ability to think and plan. It helps us strive, focus, and find things interesting."

WEBMD

The dopamine release we get from looking at pictures of cute dogs, our crushes, and food, among other things, rewards our pleasure centers with a small hit of dopamine. In fact, the average amount of time spent on Instagram is one hour and fifteen minutes per day.[36]

---

36 Amy He, "Average Time Spent on Social Media Declines," *eMarketer,* Jun 10, 2019.

But is it really anything new?

We tend to forget that overconsumption of media is not anything new. Even with the social media explosion of the 2010s, US citizens still spend an average of five hours watching television per day.[37]

TV has been replaced by social media and streaming services. MTV, Comedy Central, ABC, NBC, CBS, FOX, and every other acronym have been overtaken by Instagram, Facebook, Twitter, Snapchat, and most recently TikTok and whatever new thing that is out by the time you are reading this book.

With the unconscious notion of failure to make progress resonate in our mind, it's no wonder we are sucked so deep into the rabbit hole of TikTok dances, pets of Instagram, and Facebook posts from middle school classmates.

How can we escape this? This problem has come more into the light due to the recent quarantine situation. According to Forbes, Americans are excessively eating, drinking, smoking pot, playing video games, and watching porn while quarantined.[38]

How can we rid ourselves of spending all our time on these little hits of dopamine that come from social media, TV, and eating junk food?

---

37 Felix Richter, "The Generation Gap in TV Consumption," *Statista,* Aug 19, 2019.
38 Jack Kelly, "Americans Are Excessively Eating, Drinking, Smoking Pot, Playing Video Games And Watching Porn While Quarantined," *Forbes,* April 6, 2020.

DOPAMINE DETOX

Its 1:00 a.m. on a Tuesday. I am still awake. No big deal. I don't have to catch a bus to work or beat any traffic. I should be sleeping, or at least trying to, but I'm watching YouTube videos, my generation's greatest vice.

YouTube has a weird search algorithm: you watch a video once, and it assumes you are a connoisseur of that subject and will recommend videos of that category to you.

In the sea of videos recommended to me, "How I Tricked My Brain To Like Doing Hard Things (dopamine detox)" by Better Than Yesterday caught my eye.[39] I was about to click on "Monkey Slaps Lion," but the dopamine hits that have been keeping me up all night needed some investigation.

Better Than Yesterday argues the reason why we focus on short-term things like social media, video games, streaming services, and pornography is because of a dopamine fix.

Every time we get a hit of it, we want a little more, like a drug or gambling addict.

However, the video is not quite funny enough or the game is not yet fun enough, so we keep watching or playing.

---

39   Better Than Yesterday, "How I Tricked My Brain To Like Doing Hard Things (dopamine detox)," Feb 24, 2020, YouTube video, 14:13.

Better Than Yesterday suggests a dopamine detox. Now, it's important to note the dopamine detox deals more with everyday procrastination. If you are struggling with a substance addiction like drugs or alcohol, it's best to see a specialist who can diagnose and develop a specific treatment plan for you.

Take time away from all social media, streaming services, porn, and video games, and take a break from anything you really crave that doesn't contribute to your vision. Take a walk, write, read a book, do whatever you can to stay away from these gratifying small things. You will get bored. You will reactively reach for your phone, you might even get headaches, but the goal is to cut yourself off from dopamine dependency in order to find rewards in long-term work.

If you can get a dopamine hit from achieving milestones on your long-term goals, you will have done a great job of rewiring your brain to work toward your vision.

In my case, writing a page or a chapter or even a paragraph will bring that satisfaction and feeling of accomplishment.

This is a crucial aspect that goes into legacy building. Getting dopamine hits from milestones is what will propel you forward when looking to be someone. Sometimes we just wake up one morning and decide it's time for a change. However, that idea doesn't typically break the cycle of procrastination. What we need is to develop a *conviction*. The development of a conviction can come from a *defining moment* that *triggers* the development process.

We've seen these moments come out from inspiration, desperation, opportunities, and tragedies, and you could easily make the argument for more. There are so many ways to find motivation, such as epiphanies, learning from others, or even just possessing the need for change. All these moments, and so many others, can help you find the motivation you need to develop your vision.

CHAPTER 10

MOVING FORWARD WITH VISION

AN ERA OF UNCERTAINTY AND CHANGE

It's fall 2020, and there is so much ambiguity in the air.

The US has been turned upside down politically and socially. Stay-at-home orders enacted by the government, social stigmas, and vagueness of a solution to the coronavirus have everyone worried if we will ever get through this.

Arguably the world hasn't seen this big of a change since World War I and II.

"You are all a lost generation," says Gertrude Stein.

This accusation referred to the lack of purpose or drive resulting from the horrific disillusionment felt by those who grew up and lived through the war.

The world wars changed perspective on what life was at the time. People were questioning the status quo, examining polices that didn't make sense, and challenging them.

Hundreds of thousands of African Americans that served in WWII raised the question that if they were to give their lives defending the country, shouldn't they be equal to their white counterparts?

This question ultimately led to the civil rights movement of the '60s, which led to MLK Jr.'s March on Washington and the signing of the Civil Rights Act of 1964—which prohibits discrimination on the basis of race, color, religion, sex, or national origin.

In the 2020s, this change has manifested itself in our work culture.

The forty-hour work week was established in 1914 when Henry Ford scaled the work week down from forty-eight hours to forty hours, believing that productivity would improve.[40]

He was right, and for one hundred years it seemed like there was no flaw in the logic. Until everything changed, of course.

According to the Stanford Institute for Economic Policy Research, forty-two percent of the US labor force is working full-time from home.[41]

---

40   History.com Editors, "Ford factory workers get 40-hour week," *History*, November 13, 2009

41   Azenith Smith, "Roughly 40% of Americans are working from home full time because of the pandemic," *FOX KTVU*, June 29, 2020.

In a recent poll, half of all Americans want to continue working remotely following COVID-19.[42]

For a lot of people, it would seem discretion is favored when they do their work.

"Swapping out the nine-to-five for a more agile, independent working life brings with it one other huge benefit—a channel for self-actualization," says Leah Solivan Busque, general partner at Fuel Capital.

If there is one good thing to be identified from this pandemic, the work-from-home shift created an opportunity for a large chunk of the workforce to be someone.

In the US, the average one-way commute time is 26.1 minutes, according to the U.S. Census Bureau. If you commute to a full-time, five-days-a-week job, the round trip adds up to 4.35 hours a week and over two hundred hours (nearly nine days) per year.[43]

If we can manage our time well, that time can be spent developing and working towards our vision.

UNCERTAINTY WITH VISION

You might not be sure if the vision you have in mind is necessarily the one for you. That is completely normal.

42 Kathy Morris, "ZIPPIA POLL: HALF OF AMERICAN WORKERS WOULD RATHER WORK FROM HOME FOREVER," *Zippia*, March 2020.

43 "Average One-Way Commuting Time by Metropolitan Areas," *U.S. Census Bureau*, December 7, 2017.

Starting a vision based on an assumption of yourself may not necessarily satisfy the feeling of wanting to do more. However, we need to start somewhere.

Go with your best bet, and if it turns out what you are doing is satisfying to you and working towards that vision excites and motivates you to work towards it, accelerate in that direction.

If not, gather information of what you learned from that experience and pivot towards something else you may be interested in.

The main goal is to figure out what you truly want and, using that information, to start actively building a legacy.

OPERATIONALIZING VISION

"Vision takes a different turn the way you operationalize it."
MANAGING PARTNER AT FIRESIDE HOLDINGS AND FORMER MATTRESS FIRM CEO STEVE STAGNER.

Horst Schulze, cofounder of Ritz-Carlton Hotel Company, drives this point home in a paper he wrote during an internship at a hotel.

When Horst was a young waiter in Germany, the maître d' treated the guests differently from what Horst saw in the past.

Customers were delighted that their maître d' addressed them by name, displayed enthusiasm serving them, and dressed professionally in a tuxedo.

He referred to this style as "Ladies and Gentlemen Serving Ladies and Gentlemen."[44]

The point was that if you want to be a server, you'll be treated like a server. But if you want to be treated differently, then you need to act differently.

The vision of Ritz-Carlton was based on one principle, which was to treat people like ladies and gentlemen.

Keeping the operationalization of the vision simple and basic so thousands of people can follow is key.

We saw this in the '60s with John F. Kennedy's vision to put a man on the moon. The objective was not to only put a man on the moon, but to do so with growth in technology and education in mind.

"The space effort itself, while still in its infancy, has already created a great number of new companies, and tens of thousands of new jobs. Space and related industries are generating new demands in investment and skilled personnel, and this city and this State, and this region, will share greatly in this growth," said Kennedy in his famous "Man on the Moon" speech at Rice University in 1962.[45]

This vision of getting to the moon inspired a generation of doctors, scientists, and engineers. The speech was powerful and simple.

---

44 "Gold Standards," Ritz-Carlton, accessed October 12, 2020.
45 John Kennedy, "Address at Rice University on the Nation's Space Effort," September 12, 1962.

We saw this again with Simon Sinek's *Start With Why* philosophy.

Simon's message of the *Why* being at the center of everything we do spread not because of some elaborate social media strategy, but because it "resonates with people on such a visceral level that they share it with people they love and care about."[46]

The idea that people were *inspired* and enlisted in a greater vision that people *don't buy what you do, they buy why you do it* rippled through corporations globally, and leaders and employees of these organizations were advised to understand their own *why*.

But that was the 2010s: the 2010s were the decade of the why. Move over Simon Sinek; the 2020s are the decade to be someone.

We all have some idea of who we want to be. If someone were to shake us awake at night and ask, "What is your vision!" and we could tell them in a few words, that can be very powerful for us because this would mean even amid the most confusing of times, we can look back at our vision to make the right decisions for ourselves.

For example, when I was laying in the bunk of the Green Tortoise Hostel back when I first moved to Seattle, filled with doubt about leaving the comfort of my home city, I asked myself, "If I stay here, will I grow?"

---

46   Simon Sinek, *Start With Why* (New York: Penguin Group 2011), x.

Growth, being the center of my need to be someone, has been my guidepost in life. Growth comes from challenge, and starting over was a big challenge for me, so there was growth to be found, and I moved forward.

WHAT DOES IT MEAN TO BE SOMEONE?

It's hard to fully define what it means to be someone.

If we have a set vision of who we want to be, often we are much more. Our visions are constantly evolving; what was once one thing we wanted to become, we ended up becoming more as we learned, leveraged opportunities, and failed.

When I first moved to Seattle, it never occurred to me to write a book, let alone consider seeing book author as a viable career option. When I moved to Seattle, I had a vision to be someone, still not even fully sure what that meant.

That move, however, was the seed for change. In the two years since I've been here, I've become a fighter, a protester, a dancer, a conservationist, and now an author.

"To define is to limit."

From Oscar Wilde's *The Picture of Dorian Gray,* the quote explores how when something is given a definition, it is confined to the parameters of the definition itself and limited as a result.[47]

---

47   Ed Stennett, "To define is to limit," *Ed Stennet* (blog), April 18, 2018.

You can't define what it means to be someone because you can't limit what it means to be someone.

ON A POSITIVE NOTE

There is a joke going around that 2020 was supposed to be "my year." A new decade, 2020 being a metaphor to seeing clearly.

But the year started with Iranian General Qasem Soleimani being assassinated in a US drone strike, making us wonder if we were about to start World War III.

Then the Australian Bush Fires broke out, then Kobe died, then the world went on lockdown due to COVID-19, then the economy crashed, the US experienced its largest unemployment numbers since the Great Depression, then protests caused by the killing of George Floyd broke out across hundreds of cities in the US and around the world, then more protests against police brutality followed, and then Beirut exploded.

The anticipation of what's going to happen next month is keeping everyone on edge.

Many years ago, the great British explorer George Mallory died on the north face of Mount Everest. He was asked why he wanted to climb it.

He said, "Because it is there."

2020 has been such a challenging year. For growth, we need to seek out challenge, but this year, it has found us.

2020 might not have been your year, but if you can create your vision, the 2020s could be your decade.

ABOUT THE AUTHOR

———

Adam was born and raised in Houston, Texas, with a little time spent overseas in the Middle East. He has a Bachelor's in Business Administration from the University of Houston. Adam currently resides in Seattle, Washington, where he works in technology sales, although his heart will always be in Houston. Adam is also very involved in making an impact in the world, which he has done through volunteer opportunities at the Seattle Public Library and the Ballard Community Center. He also consults NGOs so they can better fulfill their missions in the world. If you would like to reach out or get to know Adam better, visit adamarafat.com

ACKNOWLEDGMENTS

———

I'd like to thank my mom for being a pillar of support for me throughout my life, and my dad for being a beacon of inspiration.

I would also like to thank my brother, Zak, and my sisters Deena and Diana. I try my best to be a source of inspiration for all of you, I would not have worked as hard to get where I am today if it weren't for all of you.

I would like to thank my mentor Troy Willis, Director of Business Specialist at Sysco Foods. We had a mentorship agreement back in 2016 and 2017. In 2020, I reached out to him to practice my journalistic interviewing skills. He responded immediately, was happy to help, and to top it off, he bought five pre-sale copies. Thanks Troy for being a great mentor all these years and inspiring me with your story.

I would like to thank John Pingel, Director of Corporate Relations at the Steven Stagner Sales Excellence Institute of the University of Houston. His immediate response time to assist me in this book-writing journey reflects the deep care he has for developing people, whether they be his students or alumni.

I would like to thank Steve Stagner, Managing Partner at Fireside Holdings and former CEO of Mattress Firm. Steve's philosophy of helping as many people as possible was verified when he responded to my LinkedIn direct message, agreed to an interview, and gave my pre-sale campaign the momentum it needed to become a fully funded book. In addition, *operationalizing vision* was something I learned in our interview, which found its way into the subtitle.

Finally, I would like to thank Eric Koester of the Creator's Institute and Brian Bies of New Degree Press, who made our author community understand that writing a book is not a privilege for people who are already great, but rather a way for ordinary people to discover greatness.

SUPPORTER
ACKNOWLEDGMENTS

———

In the summer of 2020 I launched an Indiegogo campaign to cover the costs of this book. In thirty-seven days, we raised $5,409 from 102 contributors across five countries.

Thanks to everyone who pitched in:

Albert Ok
Alberto Gonzalez
Alejandro Hidalgo
Ali Khan Rajwani
Alvin Mei
Andreina Rondon
Andrew Cantu
Anh-Minh Nguyen
Annam Huynh
Anne Yu
Anthony Nguyen
Antonio Del Pozo

Ashley Collins
Bradley Mosier
Brandon Bolling
Cameron Cruz
Cameron Lahay
Carl A Herman
Carlos Reyes
Chiedu Innocent
Chris McMillen
Christian Diaz
Colin Pate
Colton Ronk

Connor Hollis

Daniel Adaramola

Danny Maccio

Eduardo Robles

Eli Levy

Emma Armer

Ennis Dakhil

Eric Koester

Garrett Wesley Adams

George Watkins

Hasan Tai

Henry B Augustine

Hoc Nguyen

Ike Ukazu

Inhaeng heo

Isabel Lim

James R. Webb

Jesus Rivera

Jim Wetherbe

Joe Blount

John Pingel

Jonathan D Thomas

Jonathan Frishman

Joy Yang

Juan Bautista

Kaeem Ali

Katarina Perez

Kelly Arafat

Kevin Ramos

Lameese Taha

Lane Tunstall

Lazaro Sanchez

Leonardo Castellanos

Mariana Molina

Mario Cosbert

Mark Enriquez

Mark Jourdan Caparas

Marzanul Haque

Matthew Davies

Michael del monte

Michael George

Michael Whitaker

Michael Worotikan

Michelle Yang

Mohamed Elmadni
(Elhoderi)

Naeem Maknojia

Naomi Cosman

Nicholas D'Souza

Nicholas Neys

Ozzie Rocha

Parker Lawson

Purushothaman
Padmanabhan

Rachel Yang

renew.jon

Rhea Canas

Rick McIntyre

Ron Garza

Sammy Abbas

Saqib Arfan

Sean Williams

Seong Min Choi

Shamez Pirani

Sofiane Cherif
Spencer Cutright
Steve Stagner
Steven Ray Slover
Taylor Chan
Thomas Berry
Thomas Berry
Timothy Grant
Troy Willis
Zach Munroe

Tu Vo
Ty Anthony Hoang
Tyler Erickson
Tyler To
Ulises Tovar
Victoria Gomes
Yann Kouame
Zac Gannett

APPENDIX

INTRODUCTION

DOI (blog). "Remembering John Muir's Legacy on his Birthday." April 21, 2017. Accessed October 10, 2020. https://www.doi.gov/blog/remembering-john-muirs-legacy-his-birthday

FitzGerald, Frances. "A Reporter at Large: The Castro – I." *The New Yorker*, July 21, 1986. p. 34–70.

Kusisto, Laura. "Investors Are Buying More of the U.S. Housing Market Than Ever Before." *Wall Street Journal*, June 6, 2019. https://www.wsj.com/articles/investors-are-buying-more-of-the-u-s-housing-market-than-ever-before-11561023120

Leyland, Winston. *Out in the Castro: Desire, Promise, Activism.* San Francisco: Winston Leyland, 2001

Marquis Leinbarch, Amy. "A Mountain Calling." *National Parks Magazine*, Fall 2007. https://web.archive.org/web/20110727131453/http://www.npca.org/magazine/2007/fall/a-mountain-calling.html

Pew Research Center. "America's Changing Religious Land-scape." Last modified May 12, 2015. https://www.pewforum.org/2015/05/12/americas-changing-religious-landscape/

Randolph, Marc. *That Will Never Work*. New York: Hatchet Book Group, 2019.

Sant, Gus V., dir. *MILK*. San Francisco, CA: Focus Features, Release date October 28, 2008.

Schwantes, Marcel. "A New Study Reveals 70 Percent of Workers Say They Are Actively Looking for a New Job. Here's the Reason in 5 Words." Inc, December 4, 2018. https://www.inc.com/marcel-schwantes/a-new-study-reveals-70-percent-of-workers-say-they-are-actively-looking-for-a-new-job-heres-reason-in-5-words.html

Sierra Club. "About the Sierra Club." Accessed October 11, 2020. https://www.sierraclub.org/about-sierra-club

Stahl, Ashley. "New Study: Millennial Women Are Delaying Having Children Due To Their Careers." *Forbes*, May, 1 2020. https://www.forbes.com/sites/ashleystahl/2020/05/01/new-study-millennial-women-are-delaying-having-children-due-to-their-careers/#2abd657b276a

CHAPTER 1

Frankl, Viktor. *Man's Search for Meaning*. Boston: Beacon Press, 2006.

CHAPTER 2

Hoffman, Dan. "Maslow - Deficiency vs. Growth Motivation." *NO NONSENSE PSYCHOLOGY* (blog). May 8, 2009. http://non-onsensepsychology.blogspot.com/2009/05/maslow-deficiency-vs-growth-motivation.html.

Gleason R.,Tracy, Anne M. Sebanc, Willard W. Hartup. "Imaginary companions of preschool children." *Psychological Development* Vol 36(4), (Jul 2000): 419-428. https://psycnet.apa.org/record/2000-07944-001

Maslow, Abraham. *Toward a Psychology of Being.* Eastford: Martino Fine Books, 2011.

Maslow, Abraham. "A Theory of Human Motivation." *Psychology Review,* 1943. https://psychclassics.yorku.ca/Maslow/motivation.htm.

Hoffman, Dan. "Maslow - Deficiency vs. Growth Motivation." *NO NONSENSE PSYCHOLOGY* (blog). May 8, 2009. http://non-onsensepsychology.blogspot.com/2009/05/maslow-deficiency-vs-growth-motivation.html.

Reis, Eric. *The Lean Startup* New York: Crown Publishing Group, 2011.

Gaddefors, Johan, and Alistair R. Anderson. "Entrepreneursheep and context: when entrepreneurship is greater than entrepreneurs." *International Journal of Entrepreneurial Behavior & Research,* Volume 23 Issue 2 (2017).

CHAPTER 3

Gallo, Carmine. "Steve Jobs and the Power of Vision." *Forbes*, January 18, 2018 https://www.forbes.com/sites/carmine-gallo/2011/01/18/steve-jobs-and-the-power-of-vision/#53c-foad9172b.

Marks, Gene. "Study: 71 percent of employees are looking for new jobs." *The Washington Post*, October 19, 2017. https://www.washingtonpost.com/news/on-small-business/wp/2017/10/19/study-71-percent-of-employees-are-looking-for-new-jobs/.

Schwarzenegger, Arnold. "My advice to graduates on overcoming obstacles during coronavirus." Instagram Video, May 17, 2020. https://www.instagram.com/p/CATvbrFgn7x/

CHAPTER 4

Schultz, Howard. *Pour Your Heart Into It*. New York: Hachete Books, 1999.

CHAPTER 5

Mann, Amar, and Tony Nunes. "After the Dot-Com Bubble: Silicon Valley High-Tech Employment and Wages in 2001 and 2008." *U.S. BUREAU OF LABOR STATISTICS*, August 2009. https://www.bls.gov/opub/btn/archive/after-the-dot-com-bubble-silicon-valley-high-tech-employment-and-wages-in-2001-and-2008.pdf

DocuSign (blog). "The History of Innovation Agreements." January 31, 2018, accessed October 12, 2020.

CHAPTER 6

Goggins, David. *Can't Hurt Me*. (Austin: Lioncrest Publishing, 2018)

CHAPTER 7

A2Z Production. "Joe Rogan - CRAZY Death Row Story by Nick Yarris." September 12, 2018. Video, 39:00. https://www.youtube.com/watch?v=Upci4Bkoruo

Harvard Health Publishing. "The Power of the Placebo Effect." Last modified August 9, 2019. https://www.health.harvard.edu/mental-health/the-power-of-the-placebo-effect

Pytka, Joe, dir. *Space Jam*. Burbank, CA: Warner Bros, November 15, 1996.

UFC – Ultimate Fighting Championship. "UFC 192: Sage Northcutt Octagon Interview & Highlights." Oct 3, 2015. Video, 2:04. https://www.youtube.com/watch?v=bklcDXRwYfI

CHAPTER 8

Aten, Jamie. "What Resilience Looks Like in Complex Trauma." *Psychology Today (blog)* April 10, 2019. https://www.psychologytoday.com/us/blog/hope-resilience/201904/what-resilience-looks-in-complex-trauma.

Fleming, John, and Robert J. Ledogar. "Resilience, an Evolving Concept: A Review of Literature Relevant to Aboriginal Research." *Canada Institutes of Health Research*, (Summer 2008): 6(2).

Karson, Michael. "Turn in the Direction of the Skid." *Psychology Today (blog)* November 9, 2013. https://www.psychologytoday.com/us/blog/feeling-our-way/201311/turn-in-the-direction-the-skid

CHAPTER 9

Better Than Yesterday, "How I Tricked My Brain To Like Doing Hard Things (dopamine detox)." Feb 24, 2020, Video, 14:13, https://www.youtube.com/watch?v=9QiE-M1LrZk.

Editors, History.com. "Ford factory workers get 40-hour week." History, November 13, 2009. https://www.history.com/this-day-in-history/ford-factory-workers-get-40-hour-week.

Harman, Dan. Rick and Morty. Season 3, episode 3, "Pickle Rick." Aired August 6, 2017, on Adult Swim.

He, Amy. "Average Time Spent on Social Media Declines." *eMarketer*, Jun 10, 2019. https://www.emarketer.com/content/average-social-media-time-spent.

Richter, Felix. "The Generation Gap in TV Consumption." *Statista*, Aug 19, 2019. https://www.statista.com/chart/15224/daily-tv-consumption-by-us-adults/.

Hybrid Tech Car (blog). "A spy who loved himself: the story of Eddie Chapman – a double agent, a smuggler, a swindler and a womanizer." Accessed October 12, 2020. https://hybridtechcar.com/2018/05/20/a-spy-who-loved-himself-the-story-of-eddie-chapman-a-double-agent-a-smuggler-a-swindler-and-a-womanizer/.

Kelly, Jack. "Americans Are Excessively Eating, Drinking, Smoking Pot, Playing Video Games And Watching Porn While Quarantined." *Forbes*, April 6, 2020. https://www.forbes.com/sites/jackkelly/2020/04/06/americans-are-excessively-eating-drinking-smoking-pot-playing-video-games-and-watching-porn-while-quarantined/#af1d651404ec.

CHAPTER 10

"Average One-Way Commuting Time by Metropolitan Areas." *U.S. Census Bureau*, Decmeber 7, 2017. Smith, Azenith. "Roughly 40% of Americans are working from home full time because of the pandemic." *FOX KTVU,* June 29, 2020. https://www.ktvu.com/news/roughly-40-of-americans-are-working-from-home-full-time-because-of-the-pandemic.

Kennedy, John. "Address at Rice University on the Nation's Space Effort." September 12, 1962. https://er.jsc.nasa.gov/seh/ricetalk.htm.

Morris, Kathy. "ZIPPIA POLL: HALF OF AMERICAN WORKERS WOULD RATHER WORK FROM HOME FOREVER." *Zippia,* March 2020. https://www.zippia.com/advice/coronavirus-remote-work-survey/.

https://www.census.gov/library/visualizations/interactive/traveltime.html.

Ritz-Carlton. "Gold Standards." Accessed October 12, 2020. https://www.ritzcarlton.com/en/about/gold-standards.

Sinek, Simon. *Start With Why*. New York: Penguin Group, 2011.

Stennet, Ed. "To define is to limit" *Ed Stennet* (blog). April 18, 2018. https://edstennett.com/blog/2018/04/28/to-define-is-to-limit/.

CPSIA information can be obtained
at www.ICGtesting.com
Printed in the USA
FSHW021702121220